Army Records
for
Family Historians

Simon Fowler
William Spencer

Miscellany of nineteenth century regimental badges (private collection).

Army Records
for
Family Historians

Simon Fowler and William Spencer

2nd edition: revised and updated by William Spencer

PUBLIC RECORD OFFICE

The National Archives

Public Record Office
Ruskin Avenue
Kew
Richmond
Surrey
TW9 4DU

© Crown Copyright 1998

ISBN 1 873 162 59 6

A catalogue card for this book
is available from the British Library

CONTENTS

ILLUSTRATIONS

PREFACE

This 1998 edition of *Army Records for Family Historians* is a significant expansion and restructuring of the previous edition with much fuller coverage of the period before 1660, medals and awards and the First and Second World Wars. Detailed case studies help to bring the records to life and demonstrate what sort of picture can be developed of the individual soldier, whether officer or rank and file. New accessions of records, notably army service records from the First World War, are fully covered to date.

Thanks are due to the usual team of Aidan Lawes, Melvyn Stainton and Millie Skinns, all of whom contributed as much work as the reviser. Additional thanks must go to Keith Bartlett, Alfred Knightbridge, Simon Fowler, Major Martin Everett, archivist of the South Wales Borderers Regimental Museum for providing further details about John Harding and to Tony and Liz Light for information about William Freke Williams.

My final thanks must go to Kate, Lucy and Alice, especially Alice as she slept peacefully by the computer while I worked, even though she was only seven weeks old when I finished writing.

August 1998

Using the PRO

Most of the records described in this guide can be consulted at the Public Record Office, Ruskin Avenue, Kew, Richmond, Surrey, TW9 4DU. The Office is open between 9.30 am and 5.00 pm Mondays, Wednesdays and Fridays, 10.00 am to 7.00 pm on Tuesdays, 9.00 am to 7.00 pm on Thursdays and 9.00 am to 5.00 pm on Saturdays. Census records are seen on microfilm at the Family Records Centre, 1 Myddelton Street, London EC1R 1UW. The PRO is closed on Sundays, public holidays, and for annual stocktaking. The PRO's website address is:

http://www.pro.gov.uk/

The Office is about ten minutes' walk from Kew Gardens Underground Station, which is on London Transport's District Line, as well as the North London Line Silver Link Metro Service. For motorists it is just off the South Circular Road (A205). There is adequate parking.

Getting access to the records is simple. You will need to obtain a reader's ticket, which is free, when you first arrive. Please bring some form of identity, such as a driving licence. If you are not a British citizen you should bring your passport.

It is possible to get photocopies of most documents you find: please ask the staff for details. There is a public restaurant and a well stocked bookshop on site. Self- service lockers are available to store your belongings. You will need a £1 coin for the lockers.

In order to protect the documents, each one of which is unique, security in the reading rooms is tight. You are only permitted to take a notebook and any notes into the reading rooms. You must also only use a pencil. Eating, drinking and of course smoking are not allowed in the reading rooms.

The PRO can be a confusing place to use. If you are new to the Office it is a good idea to allow plenty of time to find your feet. The staff are both knowledgeable and friendly, and are happy to help if you get lost. You might also want to spend a few minutes watching the introductory video which offers simple advice on how to find the records you want.

Records are normally kept together according to the department which created them. The vast majority of records which relate to the British Army are in the War Office or WO lettercode. Within the lettercode each collection, or class, of records is assigned a separate class number. Thus most War Diaries for the First World War are in class WO 95. It is these class numbers which are referred to throughout this guide.

Brief descriptions of every document (piece is the term used by the PRO) are in the class lists. Several sets of lists are available in the Research Enquiries Room and other locations. The class list gives you the exact reference of the document you want. This is what you order on the computer terminal. Occasionally in this Guide we use the full reference, which is written thus: WO 95/5467.

An increasing number of documents are available on microfilm or microfiche. Where this is the case the fact is noted in the text. You do not need to order microfilms on the computer as you can help yourself to them in the Microfilm Reading Room.

Some lists have been published by the Public Record Office. Probably the most useful of these publications is the *Alphabetical Guide to War Office and certain other Military Records preserved in the Public Record Office* (PRO Lists and Indexes LXIII, 1931, reprinted 1963).

In addition, there are various other finding aids for genealogists. The best general overview is provided by Amanda Bevan's revised *Tracing Your Ancestors in the Public Record Office* (5th edition, PRO, 1999).

The structure and development of the War Office is fully described in Michael Roper's handbook *The Records of the War Office and related departments, 1660-1964* (PRO Handbook No 29, 1998).

The War Office and its records are also described in the *Guide* (microfiche edition, PRO Publications, 1996; 1999 edition in preparation), which is arranged in three parts. Part One of the *Guide* consists of administrative histories of departments, including the War Office and its component parts (Section 704). Part Two contains a description of each class of records, including those of the War Office (lettercode WO). Part Three is an index to the other two parts. Copies of the *Guide* are available at the PRO, and also on microfiche in large reference libraries and local record offices.

Introduction - Scope
of the Guide

The Public Record Office (PRO) holds many sources of great importance to family historians who had ancestors serving in the British Army. This Readers' Guide is a revision of *Army Records for Family Historians*, published by the PRO in 1992. A number of new sections and appendixes have been added, in particular to take account of the growth of interest in records of the two world wars and the release of army service records from the First World War.

This book describes the main series of records of the War Office and other government departments which provide information about officers and soldiers who have served in the British Army. Almost all War Office records give some information about individuals, but this guide concentrates on those series containing material of greatest potential interest to the family historian.

1
ORGANIZATION OF THE ARMY

It is difficult to use military records for genealogical purposes without first gaining a very general idea of how the British Army was organized, and how this changed over the years.

1.1 Before 1660

Before the outbreak of the civil war in 1642 there was no regular standing army in England, although there had been a militia in various forms since Anglo-Saxon times. Units were raised as required for service in particular campaigns and they were often known by the names of the officers who both raised and led them. There was no central organization of these units and therefore no systematic records were created for them.

1.2 1660-1750

With the restoration of Charles II a small standing army became a permanent feature of government. Its administration was the responsibility of the secretary at war, with the help of an established bureaucracy which slowly developed into the War Office. As a result records are somewhat fuller than for the period before 1660, although sparse compared with later periods. There was also a Board of Ordnance which was responsible for the supply of armaments and the erection and maintenance of fortresses. It also controlled the gunners and engineers, who, until the early eighteenth century, were normally civilians.

Because of Parliamentary suspicion of a standing army, organization of the Army remained minimal until the 1750s. The numerical strength of the Army was fixed annually by Parliament (until 1878 in the preamble to the Mutiny Act and thereafter in the Army Act) and its peacetime strength rarely exceeded 20,000 in the eighteenth century, rising to 100,000 in the first half of the nineteenth century and 200,000 after 1855. Regiments were created and abolished as necessary. In general, regiments owed allegiance as much to their commanding officers as to the monarch and were usually known by the names of their colonels until 1751. Records relating to regiments that might be run more like private businesses are more likely to have survived with private collections than with the public records.

1.3 1751-1870

By the 1750s the regiment was established as the basic unit in the Army. In 1751 each regiment of foot, that is the infantry, was given a regimental number, in order of precedence within an elaborate hierarchy of regiments, which was used until the 1880s and informally for many years after. Lists of regiments and their numbers are given in a number of books including David Ascoli, *A Companion to the British Army, 1660-1983* (London, 1983), J M Brereton, *Guide to regiments and corps of the British Army and the regular establishment* (1985), I Hallows, *Regiments and corps of the British Army* (1991) and F C Markwell and Pauline Saul, *The family historian's enquire within* (3rd edition, Federation of Family History Societies (FFHS), 1991).

The organization of the Army, however, still remained a very loose affair. In the 1780s, after the American War of Independence, there were in effect four separate armies: the Regular army; the Board of Ordnance (which included the Royal Artillery and the Royal Engineers); the militia under the control of the Home Office; and the Volunteers which existed as a series of private clubs. A series of reforms in 1855, following damning reports of general mismanagement in the Crimean War, gave the War Office responsibility for all military matters. The pre-Crimean origins of reform are discussed in Hew Strachan's *Wellington's Legacy: Reform of the British Army, 1830-1854* (Manchester University Press, 1984). The Board of Ordnance was abolished and all its responsibilities passed to the War Office. At about the same time a number of specialist Corps - medical services, supply, transport, etc were set up to deal with functions hitherto carried out on an ad hoc or regimental basis or by civilian contractors. See chapter 14.

Ireland had its own military establishment and parallel administrative structure until the Union of Ireland with Great Britain in 1801. Records of the Army in Ireland are largely in WO 35 and CO 904 with entry books of the Muster Master General of Ireland, 1709-1823, in WO 8. The Scottish Army was also a separate establishment until 1707.

1.4 1870-1945

The Cardwell army reforms of the early 1870s radically reorganized the administration of the War Office, and in 1881 the whole structure of regiments was greatly changed. Many regiments were merged, eg the 48th and 58 Foot combined to form the Northamptonshire Regiment, and many were linked to a county, although the linking of regiments to county titles was not new and first formalized in 1782. A typical regiment would have two battalions, one serving at home which would provide fresh drafts of men for the other which was stationed abroad. Local militia forces, which had been autonomous, became the third battalion of the regiment. The use of numbers to identify foot regiments was discontinued. For a description of the organization of a regiment see section 1.5.

These reforms, however, did nothing to improve the machinery by which the Army was serviced and supplied, at home or in the field, although it is from this period that serious attention was first paid to the commissariat and to medical services. In addition, no reform was made of the Royal Artillery or cavalry regiments.

The Haldane reforms of 1907 to 1912 altered the central organization of the Army, creating a General Staff, under a chief of imperial general staff, to direct military operations. In addition, an expeditionary force of six infantry battalions and six cavalry regiments was formed. This force could be mobilized within twelve days and was the nucleus of the 'Old Contemptibles' of 1914.

The slimming down of the British Army after 1945 has led to further amalgamations and changes. These are covered in David Ascoli's book.

1.5 The Regiment

The basic unit in the British Army is the regiment. The regiments were, and are, of various types: Guards or Household troops (both Horse and Foot), Cavalry (originally divided into Horse and Dragoons) and Infantry (Foot or Line). Artillery and Engineers are discussed in chapters 5 and 6. They grew out of irregular units raised privately by noblemen and others to fight certain campaigns or battles.

An infantry regiment consisted of one or more battalions, each with a paper strength of 600-1000 men. Each battalion might have between eight and twelve companies, with a paper strength of 60, 100 or 120 men. From 1803, each battalion had two lieutenant-colonels. A company eventually came to be commanded by a captain and two subalterns, who were lieutenants or second lieutenants. Before 1871 these officers purchased their commissions. Further details about this are given in section 3.5.

Administratively a regiment came to be divided into a depot and a service arm. The depot acted as the regimental headquarters and recruited and trained men for service. Before 1881 the depot moved quite frequently within the British Isles, but rarely went overseas. Depot companies were also responsible for quelling civil disturbances at home. Locations of depots are given in the Army Lists, described in section 3.2.

During the two world wars the numbers of recruits, mainly conscripts after 1916, increased many times and numerous extra 'service' battalions were formed for each regiment. Battalions were identified by a number which could take several different forms, such as:

> 1st Dorsets (ie 1st Battalion Dorsetshire Regiment)
> 5th Grenadiers (5th Battalion Grenadier Guards)
> 1/4 East Lancs (1st Line Territorials of the 4th Battalion East Lancashire
> Regiment)

Cavalry regiments were slightly different in composition. A regiment of horse consisted of between six and eight troops of fifty men each. Each troop was commanded by a captain and subalterns. Cavalry regiments were reorganized in a similar manner to their infantry counterparts in 1922. The artillery were divided into batteries - see chapter 5.

A brief history of each regiment, together with a list of the principal campaigns and battles it fought, is given in Arthur Swinson (ed), *Register of the Regiments and Corps of the British Army* (London, 1972). Individual regimental histories may be identified from A S White's *A Bibliography of the Regiments and Corps of the British Army* (1965, reprint 1988).

1.6 Location and Records of Units

There are several ways to locate the whereabouts of a regiment or battalion. The location of each battalion is given in the Monthly Army Lists, with the exception of the period between 1914 and 1918. From 1829 the stations of army units are also listed in the monthly *United Service Journal Naval and Military Magazine* (later renamed *Colburn's United Service Magazine*).

The Monthly Returns which are in classes WO 17 and WO 73 also record the location of units. The returns in WO 17 cover the period between 1759 and 1865, those in WO 73 are for 1859 to 1914. Both classes consist of returns to the adjutant general showing the distribution of each regiment at home and abroad, and its effective strength for all ranks.

From 1866 onwards the information contained in the monthly returns has been abstracted and printed in the *Annual Returns of the Army* which were published as Parliamentary Papers and are available at Kew. Returns for 1750 and 1751 are in WO 27/1-2. A summary of returns is published in John M Kitzmiller II, *In Search of the 'Forlorn Hope': a Comprehensive Guide to Locating British Regiments and their Records, 1640 to World War One* (Salt Lake City, 1988).

Orders of battle also contain lists of units, and give their location and their place in the command structure. Those for the First World War are in WO 95/5467-5494, and those for the Second World War in WO 212. Other orders of battle from 1939 are in WO 33.

Regimental records may be held locally by regimental museums or local record offices - see appendix 4 - although much of what they have is duplicated at the PRO. Chance survivals from individual units in the Public Record Office are listed in Michael Roper's *Records of the War Office*.

1.7 Higher Command

During wartime, regrouping of regiments and other units took place for operational purposes. Although still part of their parent regiments, battalions (usually four in number) came to be grouped together to form a brigade. Three brigades together formed a division. The division was a self-contained fighting force which, during both world wars, had its own artillery and support services. During the First World War, for example, its strength was about 20,000 men of all ranks but the demands of that conflict required larger formations and two, or sometimes more, divisions were grouped together as a corps. A group of two or more corps was designated as an army. It is customary to refer to armies in capital letters, ie THIRD ARMY; to corps with Roman numerals, eg XVI Corps; and to divisions with Arabic numerals, eg 30th Division. The term corps has two different meanings: as well as being a grouping of divisions it can mean a regiment of specialized troops, such as the Royal Artillery, (Royal) Army Service Corps or Royal Engineers. An even larger formation, the Army Group, was established in the Second World War.

A simple organization chart for infantry regiments is in appendix 1.

1.8 Ranks

The Army comprised commissioned officers, usually from the wealthier classes, and other ranks, often drawn from the very poorest, including paupers and criminals. Before the First World War it was very unusual for an ordinary soldier to become an officer. Very different sets of records grew up for officers and other ranks over the years. These records are therefore treated separately in this guide.

There was no uniform set of titles for the various ranks. Those used might reflect either the type of work performed or regimental custom. A list of ranks is given in appendix 2.

2

RECORDS OF THE ARMY
BEFORE 1660

2.1 Medieval Sources

In the early Middle Ages, the feudal system obliged those holding land from the crown to perform military service, either in person or by proxy, and to raise troops to serve with them. This use of 'knight service' to raise armies died out in the early fourteenth century.

The feudal system was gradually replaced by one based on contracts or 'indentures' between the King, or others, with those who were to serve directly and raise troops to serve with them. Commissions of array and commissions to musters, authorizing lords to raise forces in the King's name or inspect troops mustered, were also issued. Useful sources in print relating to knight service include the *Books of Fees 1198-1293* and *Feudal Aids* (6 volumes for 1284-1431). *Parliamentary Writs and Writs of Military Summons* is also a useful source for names of those engaged on military service. However, original records relating to soldiers are likely to be formal, with little personal detail and normally written in Latin or Norman-French. Exchequer accounts in E 101 include wages for knights and soldiers as well as some indentures for war (see **figure 1**) and E 404 includes warrants for indentures for war and knights' fees and wages in war. Accounts may also be found in E 36, E 364 and E 358, which includes the 'Agincourt Roll' (E 358/6) recording payments to those who fought at the Battle of Agincourt in 1415. Other sources relating to knights' fees include DL 40, DL 42, E 179, E 164, E 198 and the main series of Chancery enrolments, many of which have been published in detailed summaries known as calendars. These include the Scutage Rolls in C 72 (1214-1328) which record relief from 'shield tax', the Close Rolls (C 54 - C 55), the Patent Rolls (C 66), Norman Rolls (C 64), Scotch Rolls (C 71) and Welsh Rolls (C 77). Chancery Miscellanea (C 47) includes some returns of commiserve of array (C 47/2 and 5) and indentures of war for service in Ireland (C 47/10). These records are more fully described in PRO Military

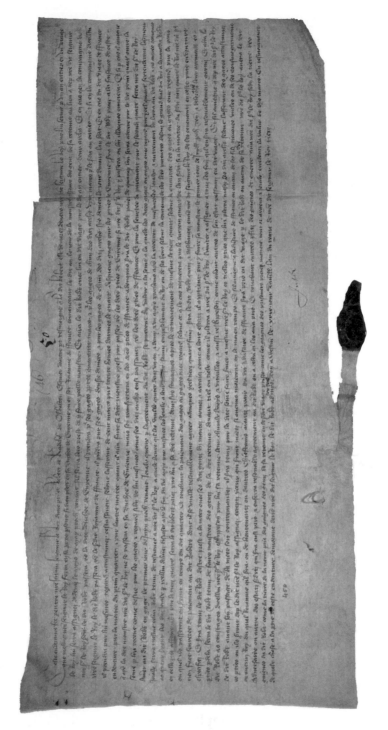

Fig 1 Indenture of Military Service of Robert de Radclyf, 1415. (E 101/69/6, no 484)

Records Information Sheet 1 *Medieval and early modern soldiers: military recruitment and service.*

2.2 Tudor and Stuart Muster Rolls and Accounts

From Anglo-Saxon times, men were liable to military service as a local home defence force. The Statute of Winchester (1285) required all those between fifteen and sixty to be assessed to equip themselves with weapons and armour, according to their means, from scythes and knives for those holding less than 40 shillings worth of land to horse and armour for the wealthiest individuals. In the sixteenth century, local Commissioners of Array, or the Lord Lieutenant of the county, assisted by local officials such as the parish constable, were responsible for making and inspecting such assessments.

Muster rolls list the names of local inhabitants who were liable to military service and the equipment they were required to have. The earliest known is from 1522, but obviously musters were held for centuries before. The rolls, or sometimes certificates of musters giving only total numbers of men, were forwarded to the Exchequer or the Privy Council, and have therefore became part of the public records.

Some muster rolls have only survived with the private papers of those local gentry families who served as commissioners of array or deputy lieutenant and these may be deposited in local record offices. The private papers of a Cheshire gentleman, John Daniel of Daresbury, held here under the reference SP 46/52, give an idea of the sort of material that can be found - correspondence and papers relating to musters and commissions, and several muster rolls of the trained band of which he was captain.

The essential guide to the present location of muster rolls is *Tudor and Stuart Muster Rolls - A Directory of Holdings in the British Isles* by J Gibson and A Dell (Federation of Family History Societies, 1991 edition). This is arranged by county, and then by hundred (a division of the county containing a number of parishes). For each county it lists what is held by the PRO, with full document references; what is held by local record offices; and what has been transcribed and published. Many publications by local record societies are held by the Public Record Office library.

Muster rolls do not represent a complete census of the male population, as a comparison with names listed in surviving taxation returns in E 179 clearly shows - it has been estimated that, on average, either muster or tax return is likely to omit one third of the names it was supposed to contain. The unfit and those too poor to provide the necessary equipment (and who might not be trusted to use their weapons in defence of property) may be omitted altogether.

Muster rolls for 1522-1547 are found in the record classes E 101/bundles 58-62 and 549; E 36/16-55a; E 315/464 and 466 and SP 1- SP 2; see **figure 2** for an example. Many are listed in *Letters and Papers of the Reign of Henry VIII*. A few from 1548 are in SP 10/3-4. For the reign of Elizabeth I (1558-1603), and especially for 1569, 1573, 1577 and 1580, muster rolls and certificates are in SP 12 and E 101/bundles 64-66. From 1570, most are not lists of men but certificates, listing the numbers of men only, grouped by hundred and according to the equipment they provided; musters listing names may only be of the 'trained bands', ie those men who were selected for special training. Musters for the reign of James I (1603-1625) are in SP 14 and for Charles I (1625-1640) in SP 16 - SP 17. Most of these State Paper classes are seen on microfilm and are well listed and indexed by printed Calendars. These records are more fully described in PRO Military Records Information Sheet 2 *Tudor and Stuart local soldiery: militia muster rolls*.

Other sources where references to individual officers and men, including applications by widows for pensions, may sometimes be found for this period include the published *Calendars of State Papers Domestic*, *State Papers Foreign*, *State Papers Ireland*, and *Privy Council Registers*, all of which are indexed by personal name. Exchequer and Audit Office accounts in E 101, E 351 and AO 1 - AO 3 may occasionally list the names of individuals serving in particular campaigns and the 'licences to pass beyond the seas' in E 157 record oaths of allegiance by soldiers serving abroad, notably in the Low Countries.

2.3 The English Civil War

Although there are no individual military service records as such for this period, it can be possible to identify individual soldiers in the State Papers and in numerous accounts, but no comprehensive indexes of names exist for these records. There is a useful overview of the sources in M Bennet's 'All embarqued in one button: an introduction to sources for soldiers administrations and civilians in civil war Britain and Ireland', *Genealogists' Magazine* (December 1996), vol 25, no 8.

Edward Peacock's *Army Lists of the Roundheads and Cavaliers* (London, 1863), a reprint of a contemporary pamphlet, is arranged by regiment and lists officers only in the royalist and parliamentary forces in 1642. Royalist officers can also be found

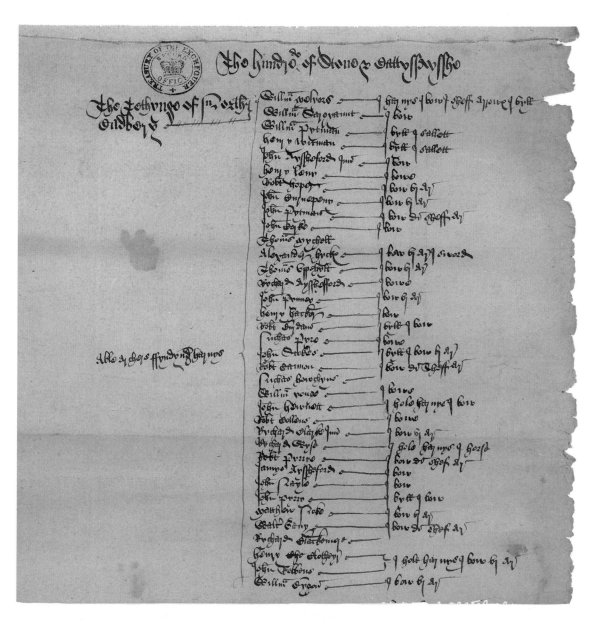

Fig 2 Tudor muster roll. Extract from a muster roll of 1539 - for the tithing of North Cadbury in the hundred of Stone and Catsash in Somerset. (E 101/59/21)

through the personal name indexes to the printed *Calendars of State Papers Domestic*; *Calendar of the Committee for Compounding with Delinquents* (delinquents being royalists who were fined); and the *Calendar of the Committee for the Advance of Money*. An article by P R Newman, 'The Royalist Officer Corps 1642-1660' *Historical Journal*, XXVI (1983), describes other sources, including *Docquets of Letters Patent 1642-6*, ed W H Black (1837) which lists commissions granted by King Charles I to raise regiments and appoint senior officers. Such senior officers usually made their own personal appointments of junior officers in their regiments, reference to which may sometimes be found in private papers. A few isolated examples of commissions issued by Prince Rupert are in C 115/126/6515-6517. After the Restoration of Charles II in 1660, many royalists petitioned the King for rewards for loyalty to his father and such petitions appear in the printed *Calendars of State Papers Domestic* for his reign. A special fund was set up to reward officers who had seen military service and a list of over 5,000 names was printed and indexed in the 1663 *List of Officers Claiming to the Sixty Thousand Pounds* (SP 29/68, ff 42-107). An article by P R Newman, 'The 1663 List of Indigent Royalist Officers', *Historical Journal*, 30 (1987) discusses the value of this source. Another list of soldiers of the rank of mayor and above of the same date is SP 29/159, no 45.

An initial search for Parliamentary officers is also best made in printed sources such as R R Temple's 'The Original Officer List of the New Model Army', *Bulletin of the Institute of Historical Research*, LIX (1986) for 1645; Anne Lawrence's *Parliamentary Army Chaplains 1642-1651* (Royal Historical Society, 1990); C H Firth and G Davies' *The Regimental History of Cromwell's Army* (Oxford, 1940) and *The New Model Army* by Ian Gentles (Blackwell, 1992). The *Calendars of State Papers Domestic* draw on the State Papers (SP 16 - SP 17) and records of the Council of State (SP 18 and SP 25), and the Committee of Both Kingdoms (SP 21), amongst other sources, and may also prove a fruitful source of names.

For ordinary Parliamentary soldiers, speculative searches in accounts and other records of payments are time-consuming but may be rewarding. The Commonwealth Exchequer Papers in SP 28, which are not included in the printed *Calendars*, contain warrants, accounts, certificates, testimonials and muster rolls, with numerous references to individuals, but there are no indexes and most are arranged topographically, eg SP 28/265 contains a muster of the 55 officers and men of Captain Hicke's cavalry troop and list of 'distressed widowers whose husbands were slaine in the service. SP 28/142 has a number of regimental lists c 1649-1650 purporting to bear the signatures of officers and men in certain regiments and appointing representatives to negotiate for pay arrears. Other accounts, mainly relating to payments to officers, are in E 101, E 315, E 351, WO 47, WO 49, WO 54 and WO

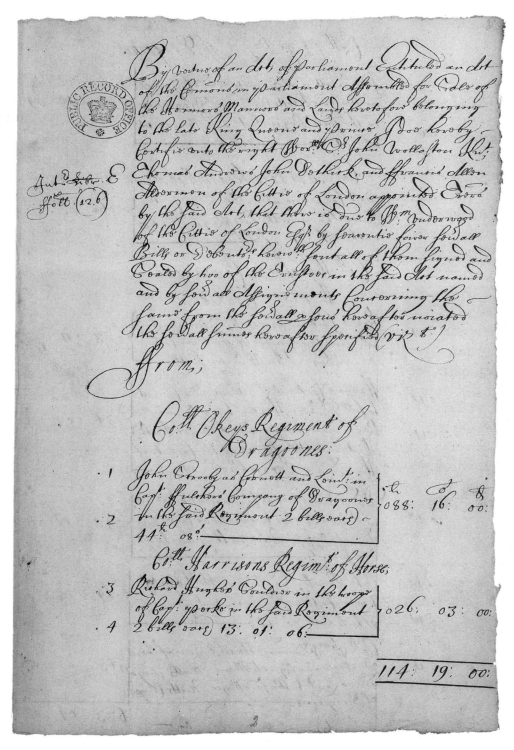

Fig 3 Arrears of pay owing to Cornet John Scrooby and Trooper Richard Hughes, 1652. (E 121/3, no 3)

55. Arrears of pay owing to soldiers that were to be secured on the sale of crown lands (in England and Wales only) are recorded in E 121. These contain thousands of names and identify the company and troop and regiment in which a man served, but they are not indexed and are arranged by the county in which the property was situated. An example is illustrated as **figure 3**. As well as the basic accounts, there are a few examples of certificates of entitlement issued to individual soldiers. Similar debentures were issued to soldiers who had served in Ireland and were granted confiscated Irish lands but these records, which were kept in Dublin, have not survived. There is a calendar of some of the grants of land that were confirmed after 1660, with an index of names, in the *Fifteenth Report* of the Irish Record Commission (1825). Further references to men, mainly officers, who served in Ireland, may be found in the *Calendars of State Papers Ireland*.

Muster rolls for the Scots Army in England in 1646, arranged by regiment, are in SP 41/2.

A little used source, that may give a brief service history, is the records of the Committee for Indemnity in SP 24, set up to protect soldiers from legal actions arising out of their military service during the fighting, eg SP 24/31 has the case of Issac Appleton, an apprentice tailor who was sued by his master for breaching his apprenticeship contract by leaving to serve with the parliamentary forces in 1643. Cases are arranged in alphabetical sequence and there are indexed order books. These records are further described in Military Records Information Sheet 3 *Civil War Soldiers*.

3
COMMISSIONED OFFICERS

3.1 Introduction

To trace the service record of an officer in the Army you need to know his regiment, because the War Office kept no continuous central record of officers.

The most important source for the career of an officer in the Army is the printed Army Lists. If your ancestor does not appear in these lists it is very unlikely that he was an officer. The Army Lists have been produced since 1740. They are arranged by regiment, and normally indexed after 1867.

There are two main types of service record, those created by the War Office, which are in WO 25, and those produced by the regiments themselves, which are in WO 76. There are incomplete card indexes to these records in the Research Enquiries Room at Kew. Further information about them is in section 3.6.

Records giving personal information about an army officer were created routinely upon the granting of a commission, promotion, resignation or his being placed upon the half-pay list, and occasionally at other stages in his career.

There were four sorts of commissioned officer:

1. General officers, who co-ordinated the efforts of the whole army. They had the rank of field marshal, general, lieutenant general and major general.
2. Field officers, who commanded a regiment; that is, colonel, lieutenant colonel and major.
3. Company officers, who were in charge of units within a regiment; that is, captain (in command of a company) and his subalterns, lieutenant, cornet (in the cavalry), ensign (infantry). In 1871 cornets and ensigns became second lieutenants.
4. Others: paymasters, adjutants, quartermasters, surgeons and chaplains.

There were also some other ranks, such as brigadier general, colonel-commandant, and brigade-major. Officers were graded by seniority, which ruled promotion within the regiment. Brevet officers were officers who were raised to the next rank in name only, but with first refusal on the next substantive rank. Some officers held two ranks at the same time: the regimental rank, which was higher and was usually a special appointment, and the army rank, which was the actual rank of his commission. This often occurred during the two world wars when vacancies at a higher rank had to be filled because of casualties.

A list of Army ranks is in appendix 2.

There are numerous printed sources listing officers by name and identifying their regiments.

3.2 Army Lists

The broad outline of an officer's career should be fairly easy to discover from the official Army Lists.

Brief details of army officers have been gathered together since 1702 and published in regular series from 1754. Sets may be available in large reference libraries, although the earliest volumes are very rare. Incomplete printed sets are available at Kew but there are also complete record sets, with manuscript amendments, of the annual lists between 1754 and 1879, and of the quarterly lists from 1879 to 1900, in WO 65 and WO 66 respectively. The manuscript lists up to 1765 are indexed by name. WO 65/164-168 includes special lists of forces in North America, 1778; British-American half-pay officers, 1782 and Foreign Corps, 1794-1802.

There are five distinct series of Army Lists:

1. **Annual Army Lists** date from 1754 to 1879 and are arranged by regiment. Volumes from 1766 are indexed. Engineer and artillery officers are included in the index from 1803 only. The series was replaced by a Quarterly Army List from June 1879 - see **figure 4**.

2. **Monthly Army Lists** date from 1798 to June 1940 and are arranged by regiment. In addition, they include some idea of the location of each unit. Officers of colonial, militia and territorial units are included. The lists are indexed from 1867. After July 1939 the lists were given a security classification and not published and in 1940 they were replaced by the Quarterly Army List.

229	230	231

Line Battalions.

229

5 F.—continued.

Frederic R. Carleton 13July67
Chas. Herbert Broad, *I.of M.*
                                   12Oct.67
Charles Hackett 16Oct.67
2W. FitzAllan Way 22Aug.68
2Josiah W. Pearse-Hobbs,
  I. of M. 3Feb.69
1Geo.Wm.Hargreave,*d.* 27Feb.69
2H. Aitken Cherry, *adj.* 27Feb.69
2Fred. Wm. Saunders 5Jan.70
1Geo. Hart Dyke 19Jan.70
1Edw. Le M. Trafford 9Apr.70
1Henry Kilgour 8June70
2Chas. Geo. Heathcote 36Nov.70
2Reginald H. Thurlow 24Dec.70
1James Sinclair Cramsie 22Feb.71
2Robt. Milnes Thornton 22Mar.71
1Herbert Reay Gall 6Oct.71
2Middleton W. Biddulph 28Oct.71
2Richard Williamson 28Oct.71
1Samuel Boxwell 28Oct.71
2Robt. Auld 28Oct.71
1Thos. Arthur Campion 28Oct.71
1Alexr. Chancellor, *d.* 28Oct.71
2Percy Fra. Lambart 28Oct.71
2Harris England Buchanan
                                   28Oct.71
2Hen. Hanbury Davies 28Oct.71
2Chas. L. S. Auber 28Oct.71
1Geo. Nevile Wyatt 28Oct.71
1Chas. G. C. Money 29May72
2Hen. Mordaunt Matthew 3July74

Sub Lieutenants.

1Hen. Beaufoy Thornhill 23Apr.73
1Geo. Atkins Collins 13June74

Paymasters.

1Fred. Blanco Forster, *m.* 5Dec.51
                                   lt. 13Oct.48
2Joshua J. Bowness 14Oct.68
                                   21Aug.67

Instrs. of Musk.

2J. W. Pearse-Hobbs, *lt.* 13May72
1C. H. Broad, *lt.* 25Apr.73

Adjutants.

1W. S. Darley, *lt.* 5Aug.67
2H. A. Cherry, *lt.* 26June72

Quar. Masters.

1Fra. Drake 17Nov.57
2Michael Downey 4Oct.73

Medical Officers.

1A. M. Tippetts, *sur. m.* 15June66
2C. F. Pollock, *M.B., sur.*

Scarlet—Facings bright green.

Ag. Messrs. Cox & Co.
Ir.Ag. Sir E. Borough, *Bt. & Co.*

230

6th (Royal First Warwick-
shire).

1 Bn. ....*Bengal,*
  Dep. ....*with 2 Bn.*
2 Bn. ....*Guernsey.*
Brigade, Sub-District and } 28
Brig. Dep.† (*Warwick*)
  († *Not yet formed.*)

The Antelope.
The Rose and Crown.

"Roleia." "Vimiera."
"Corunna." "Vittoria."
"Pyrenees." "Nivelle."
"Orthes." "Peninsula."
"Niagara."

Colonel.

John ffolliott Crofton, *l.g.*
                                   5Sept.69

Lt. Colonels.

Chas. O. Creagh-Osborne,
  C.B. *c.*, *p.s.c.*, *s.* 1Feb.67
2John H. F. Elkington, *c,* 27Nov.67
1Thos. Lynden Bell 1Apr.73

Majors.

2Henry B. Feilden 8June67
2Jas. N. Colthurst 30Aug.71
1Evan B. Gardyne 1Feb.73
1Wilsone Black, *p.s.c.* 1Apr.73

20 Captains.

2Lewis Blyth Hole, *m.* 29Sept.59
1Alfred Austin, *m., d.* 30Apr.61
2D. G. Protheroe 28Jan.62
1Wm. C. Wolseley 19Dec.62
1Dawson K. Evans 29May63
2Spencer Field 22Mar.64
2Jas. Geo. Cockburn 3May64
2Charles Whyte 9Mar.66
2H. Burrows Adcock 3July66
1Douglas Hastings, *l.c.* 15Mar.53
1Albert H. Harrison 8June67
1Chas. W. H. Wilson 14Sept.67
2Fredk. Helyar 14Oct.68
1Jas. FitzGerald 17Mar.69
2Jas. T. Nugent 19Jan.70
2Alex. C. Hall 28May70
1Jacob B. Hopkins 1Apr.73
2Hen. P. L'E. St. George
                                   20Oct.69
1Wm. Grant, *s.* 24Sept.74
1Gust. W. B. Collis 27Feb.75

Lieutenants.

2Arthur Morton 19Dec.62
2Adol. R. A. Collis 1Dec.65

231

6 F.—continued.

2Geo. Sharp Grimble 9Mar.66
1David M. F. Brady 29May67
2Jas.Ruddle Gibbs,*I.of M.* 8June67
1Gerald de Courcy Morton
                                   13July67
1Robert Stratford 2Aug.65
1Aug. Wm. Whitworth, *I.of M.*
                                   14Sept.67
1Fred. Leigh Grundy 9Nov.67
2James Lewis, *adj.* 30Sept.68
1Richard Meredith 17Mar.69
2Hen. Deering Thomas 29May69
1Frank Longbourne 28May70
2Neville Fredk. Mansergh
                                   27Oct.71
2Gerald H. C. Stracey 28Oct.71
1Edward Arthur Ball 28Oct.71
1Arthur M. O'Beirne 28Oct.71
1Richd. John Doyne 28Oct.71
2Denman Croft Murray 28Oct.71
1Edwd. H. Corse-Scott 28Oct.71
1E. J. Winnington-Ingram
                                   28Oct.71
2Willoughby E.G. Forbes 28Oct.71
1Hen. Blake Harward 28Oct.71
Chas. Boileau Down (prob.)
                                   28Oct.71
1St. Geo.John Rathborne 28Oct.71
1Thos. Geo. Lumsden 15Jan.73
2Thos. R. F. B. Hallowes 12Nov.73
2John Wm. Stevenson 2Dec.74

Sub Lieutenants.

1Valens C. Tonnochy 9Aug.73
2Wm. Erskine Scott 9Aug.73
2Gregory Haines 9Aug.73
2Gilbert M. Yaldwyn 9Aug.73
2Morey Quayle Jones 12Nov.73
1Hen. Lushington Ramsay
                                   28Feb.74
1Wm. Conrad Faithfull 21Sept.74
1Chas. Edwd. Pollock 11Feb.75

Paymasters.

2†John O'Connor, *m.* 3Nov.57
                       qua. mast. 11Mar.53
1Wm. Wastell, *m.* 21Dec.60
                                   lt. 26Jan.58

Instrs. of Musk.

2J. R. Gibbs, *lt.* 30Aug.70
1A. W. Whitworth, *lt.* 25Mar.71

Adjutants.

2J. Lewis, *lt.* 21Aug.72

Quarter Masters.

1Geo. Beedle 10July66
2Jas. B. Tippetts 4Oct.73

Medical Officers.

2F. J. Shortt, *sur. m.* 4Feb.71
1E. F. O'Leary, *M.D., sur. m.*
                                   9Sept.71

Scarlet—Facings blue.

† *On duty in 66th Sub-Dist.*

Ag. Messrs. Cox & Co.
Ir.Ag. Sir E. Borough, *Bt. & Co.*

Fig 4 The Official Army List, 6th Foot, 1875.

3. **Quarterly Army Lists** There are two separate series of quarterly lists:

1879-1922. These lists have two distinctive features. Firstly, in addition to the regimental list (which was discontinued in 1908) they include a gradation list; that is, lists of officers in seniority order, with dates of birth and promotions. In addition, from April 1881 details of officers' war service are included. Between 1909 and 1922 these details appear in the January issue only. This series of the Quarterly List was replaced by Half Yearly Army Lists in 1923.

July 1940 - December 1950. Quarterly Army Lists were produced in place of the Monthly Army List from July 1940. They were classified documents and not published. Despite the new name, the lists continued to be produced monthly or bi-monthly until December 1943. From then on they were issued quarterly until January 1947. They are not regimental lists and do not include the gradation list or details of officers' war services. From April 1947, although still styled the Quarterly Lists, they were published in April, August and December each year.

4. **Half Yearly Army Lists** exist for the period between 1923 and February 1950. They replaced and took a similar form to the Quarterly Army Lists. They were issued in January and July each year and included a gradation list of serving officers. The January issue also includes a list of retired officers. From 1939 they became a restricted publication. From 1947 they were issued annually in February.

5. **Army Lists and Army Gradation Lists** The Army List was revised in 1951, and now consists of three parts: part 1, a list of serving officers; part 2, a list of retired officers; part 3, a brief biography of officers called the Gradation List. Part 3 is a restricted publication, and is not available to the general public. Part 2 is now published only every four years.

3.3 Other Lists

Details of officers granted commissions before 1727, compiled from State Papers and other PRO sources, can most easily be traced in Charles Dalton, *English Army Lists and Commission Registers, 1661-1714* (6 vols, London, 1892-1904, reprinted by Francis Edwards, 1960) and *George I's Army, 1714-1727* (2 vols, London, 1910-1912). Copies of Dalton's books are available at Kew. You may also find useful:

The Military Register, published from 1768 to 1772 and in 1779, which includes Army and marine officers.

The Royal Military Calendar, published in 1820, which contains service records for officers from field marshal down to major, who held the rank at the date of publication. The *Calendar*, however, contains no personal information or details of officers' families. These books are available at Kew.

Lieutenant General Henry Hart started an unofficial army list in February 1839, in part to fulfil the need for a record of officers' war services which he felt were inadequately covered in the official Army List. He noted them meticulously in extensive footnotes. *Hart's Army Lists* cover the period between 1839 and 1915 and were issued quarterly. An annual volume which contained additional information was also published. Hart's own copies of his Army Lists, 1839-1864, with material used by compile them, are in WO 211. An incomplete set of Hart's lists between 1840 and 1882 is available on open shelf in the Research Enquiries Room. Certain volumes have been reprinted by the Naval and Military Press. An example is reproduced as **figure 5**.

Lists of artillery officers were published in *List of Officers of the Royal Regiment of Artillery, 1716 - June 1914* (3 vols, London, 1899, 1914). A similar list was compiled for the Royal Engineers: *Roll of Officers of the Corps of Royal Engineers from 1660 to 1898* (London, 1898). In addition, there is a published *List of Commissioned Medical Officers of the Army, 1660-1960* (2 vols, 1925, 1968). These books are available at Kew.

General staff officers and War Office staff (including civilian employees) are listed in the *War Office List* published by the War Office itself between 1861 and 1964.

A few manuscript lists of army officers between 1702 and 1823 may be found in WO 64 and there is a manuscript index to entries in the Army Lists between 1704 and 1765 in the Research Enquiries Room.

3.4 Commissions, Appointments, Transfers and Promotions

Officers held their rank by virtue of a royal commission. The issue of a commission, or warrant of appointment, is likely to be recorded in several places. A small collection of original commissions between 1780 and 1874 is in WO 43/1059. Appointments and promotions of officers were announced in the *London Gazette* (hence the term 'gazetting') and, from 1829, in the *United Service Journal and Naval and Military Magazine*.

	Lieutenant-Colonels.	CORNET, ETC.	LIEUT.	CAPTAIN.	MAJOR.	LIEUT.-COLONEL.	WHEN PLACED ON HALF PAY.
🅟 🅱🅰	Wm. Henry Elliott, KH., *Lt.-Col.*, 51 Foot	6 Dec. 09	13 Aug. 12	9 Nov. 20	12 July 31	27 June 38	
	Peter Edwards, *Major*, Unattached	1 Oct. 07	3 June 09	17 Mar. 11	13 May 24	28 June	11 May 26
🅟	William Freke Williams, KH.,[134] *Major*, Unattached, *Assistant Adjutant-General at Athlone*	30 Aug. 10	10 June 11	31 Oct. 14	9 April 25	do	
🅟 🅱🅰	William Cartwright,[135] *Major*, Unattached...........	2 July 12	6 Jan. 14	16 Nov. 20	19 May	do	19 May 25
🅟 🅱🅰	John Garland, KH.,[136] *Major*, do.	14 Mar. 05	4 Nov. 06	26 Nov. 13	26 May	do	26 May 25
	William Miller, KH., *Major*, h. p. Royal Artillery	1 Oct. 01	13 June 03	1 Feb. 08	27 May	do	29 Aug. 26
🅟	John Campbell, *Lt.-Col.*, on retired full pay, 97 Foot......	9 July 03	17 Mar. 04	5 May	do	do	
🅟	Hardress Robert Saunderson,[139] *Major*, Unattached.......	15 June 04	18 Feb. 06	do	do	do	30 Sept. 26
	Wm. Henry Newton, KH., *Lt.-Col.*, R. Can. R. Regt. ...	20 Dec. 00	25 June	do	do	do	
	Nicholas Lawson Darrah, *Lt.-Col.*, 97 Foot	16 Aug. 04	2 April 05	30 June	do	do	
🅰🅱	Arthur Gore,[140] *Major*, Unattached.....................	22 Dec. 04	10 Oct. 05	14 July	do	do	4 May 26
🅟	David Goodsman, *Major*, do.	12 Aug. 99	23 Mar. 00	28 Nov.	do	do	1 June 26
	Loftus Owen, *Major*, do.	22 Dec. 99	1 Nov. 02	8 Dec.	do	do	10 June 26
	Pringle Taylor, KH.,[142] *Major*, do.	15 Aug. 11	2 July 12	2 Jan. 20	16 June	do	4 July 34
🅣🅱	Thomas Robert Swinburne, *Major*, Unattached	24 June 13	never	26 Dec. 16	10 Sept.	do	10 Sept. 25
🅟 🅱🅰	George Whichcote,[144] *Major*, do.	10 Jan. 11	8 July 12	22 Jan. 18	29 Oct.	do	29 Oct. 25
🅱🅰	James Arthur Butler,[145] *Major*, do.	23 Jan. 13	never	18 April 16	19 Nov.	do	19 Nov. 25
	Joseph Kelsall, *Lt.-Col.*, on retired full pay, 70 F.	17 Dec. 03	21 Feb. 05	11 Nov. 13	23 Nov. 32	do	
	Richard Wm. Astell, *Capt. & Lt.-Col.*, Gren. Guards.....	never	20 Nov. 23	15 Sept. 27	never	7 July	
	Robert Spark, *Lt.-Col.*, 83 Foot	May 07	3 Sept. 07	17 Feb. 20	25 Dec. 35	28 July	
🅟	George Maunsell,[147] *Lt.-Col.*, Unattached...............	13 Mar. 06	25 Dec. 06	18 July 11	21 Nov. 28	15 Sept.	12 May 43
	P. F. Wellesley Campbell, *Capt. & Lt.-Col.*, Scots Fus. Gds...	13 Jan. 25	14 July 25	3 July 29	never	9 Nov.	
	Thomas Henry Johnston, *Lt.-Col.*, 66 Foot	21 Feb. 22	1 Oct. 25	24 Oct. 26	20 May 36	28 Dec.	
	Henry Aitchison Hankey, *Lt.-Col.*, 1 Dr. Guards	26 June 23	10 Mar. 25	15 Aug. 26	27 Sept. 33	1 Mar. 39	
🅱🅰	John Campbell, *Major*, Unattached................	23 Jan. 12	28 Mar. 14	2 April 18	22 April 20	20 Mar.	4 Sept. 43
	Plomer Young, KH., *Lt.-Col.*, do., *Assist. Adj.-Gen. in Canada*	8 May 05	3 Sept. 06	20 April 15	12 Feb. 28	do	1 Sept. 40
	Henry Dive Townshend, *Lieut.-Col.*, Unattached.........	16 July 12	14 Sept. 15	1 Nov. 21	10 Oct. 35	do	28 April 46
	James Bucknall Bucknall Estcourt,[143] *Lt.-Col.*, Unatt.	13 July 20	9 Dec. 24	4 Nov. 25	21 Oct. 36	do	25 Aug. 43
	George Phillpotts, *Lt.-Col.*, Royal Engineers	1 May 11	7 June 11	23 Mar. 25	28 June 38	do	
	Thomas Wright, CB., *Lieut.-Col.*, 39 Foot	18 Dec. 12	22 April 14	14 July 25	12 Mar. 37	24 April	
	Frederick Charles Griffiths, *Lt.-Col.*, Unatt., *Assistant Commandant at Maidstone*	17 June 24	10 Feb. 26	5 April 31	28 Oct. 37	3 May	3 May 39
	William Blois, *Lt.-Col.*, 52 Foot, on retired full pay	3 May 15	30 Aug. 21	14 July 25	12 Aug. 34	11 May	

134 Lieut.-Colonel W. F. Williams served in Senegal, Goree, and Sierra Leone during 1811 and 12; and in the Peninsula from Aug. 1813 to the end of that war, including San Sebastian, the passage of the Bidassoa, battles of Nivelle and Nive (11th, 12th, and 13th Dec.), and the investment of Bayonne. He embarked for Bordeaux in 1814 with the expedition to the Chesapeak under General Ross, and was wounded at the battle of Bladensburg, first slightly in the left arm, and again severely by a musket-ball through the left shoulder. He served subsequently for several years in the West Indies; and he was sent on a particular service to Canada during the insurrection in that country in 1838 and 39.

135 Lieut.-Colonel Cartwright served the campaigns of 1813 and 14 with the 61st, including the battles of the Pyrenees, Nivelle, Nive, Orthes, and Toulouse. Served the campaign of 1815 with the 10th Hussars, and was present at the battle of Waterloo.

Fig 5 *Hart's Army List*, William Freke Williams, 1849.

Warrants for the issue of commissions, between 1679 and 1782, can be found in the military entry books in the State Papers (SP 44/164-203) which are continued from 1782-1855 for Militia commissions in HO 51.

Commission books between 1660 and 1803, are in WO 25/1-121. Similar information can be found in the notification books, 1704-1858 (WO 4/513-520, WO 25/122-203).

Appointments and subsequent transfers and promotions are also recorded in the succession books of the secretary at war. They were compiled retrospectively from the notification and commission books. They are in two series:

by regiments	1754-1808	(WO 25/209-220)
by date	1773-1807	(WO 25/221-229).

Original submissions and entry books of submissions to the sovereign of recommendations for staff and senior appointments, rewards for meritorious service, and for commissions and appointments, 1809, 1871-1914, are in WO 103.

For artillery and engineer officers see chapters 5 and 6.

3.5 Purchase of Commissions

Before 1871 many commissions (up to the rank of colonel) were purchased, although in time of war there were opportunities for promotion by ability. There were set prices for commissions, but they were widely exceeded, especially in fashionable regiments such as the foot guards. Once a commission had been purchased, officers were then able to buy up to the next rank as the opportunity presented. The whole system was widely condemned during the mid-Victorian period, and was finally abolished in 1871 by the Army Purchase Commission The system is fully described in Anthony Bruce's *The Purchase System in the British Army, 1660-1871* (London, 1980). However, pay for officers remained relatively poor and in many regiments, even in the twentieth century, many officers had private means as well as army pay. Officers continued to be drawn largely from the upper strata of society.

Applications to purchase and sell commissions, between 1793 and 1870, are in the Commander-in-Chief's memoranda in WO 31. Accompanying correspondence may also be included; examples are given in G Hamilton-Edwards, *In Search of Army Ancestry*. These records are arranged chronologically by the date of appointment or promotion, usually in monthly bundles. These applications may shed considerable extra light on the individual concerned. The supporting documents often contain statements of service, certificates of baptisms, marriages, deaths and burials (some of which have been removed to WO 42), and letters of recommendation. For an example see **figure 6**.

Correspondence about the purchase and sale of commissions between 1704 and 1858 is contained in a series of indexed letter books in WO 4/513-520.

Hart's Army Lists note whether an officer bought his commission or not, and give the date when the purchase was made. Using this information it is thus possible to discover which bundle in WO 31 is likely to contain details of the purchase. Both the official Army Lists and Hart's Army Lists record when an officer sold his commission. Unfortunately an exact date is not given, but the month or quarter can be determined.

Registers of service of every officer holding a commission on 1 November 1871 are in the papers of the Army Purchase Commission in WO 74, together with a series of applications from officers on the British and Indian establishments, 1871-1891, to which certificates of service are attached. Papers and applications are indexed by regiment but not by name of applicant.

3.6 Records of Service

Records of service of officers held by the Public Record Office fall into two main groups: those compiled by the War Office and those compiled in regimental record offices.

The records described below are only for officers who had retired before the end of 1913. Records of service of officers who served in the First World War and later wars and campaigns are described in chapters 16-18.

3.6.1 War Office returns of service

The War Office did not begin to keep systematic records of officers' service until the early nineteenth century, having relied on records retained by regimental record offices. During the nineteenth century, however, the War Office compiled five series of statements of service based on returns made by officers themselves:

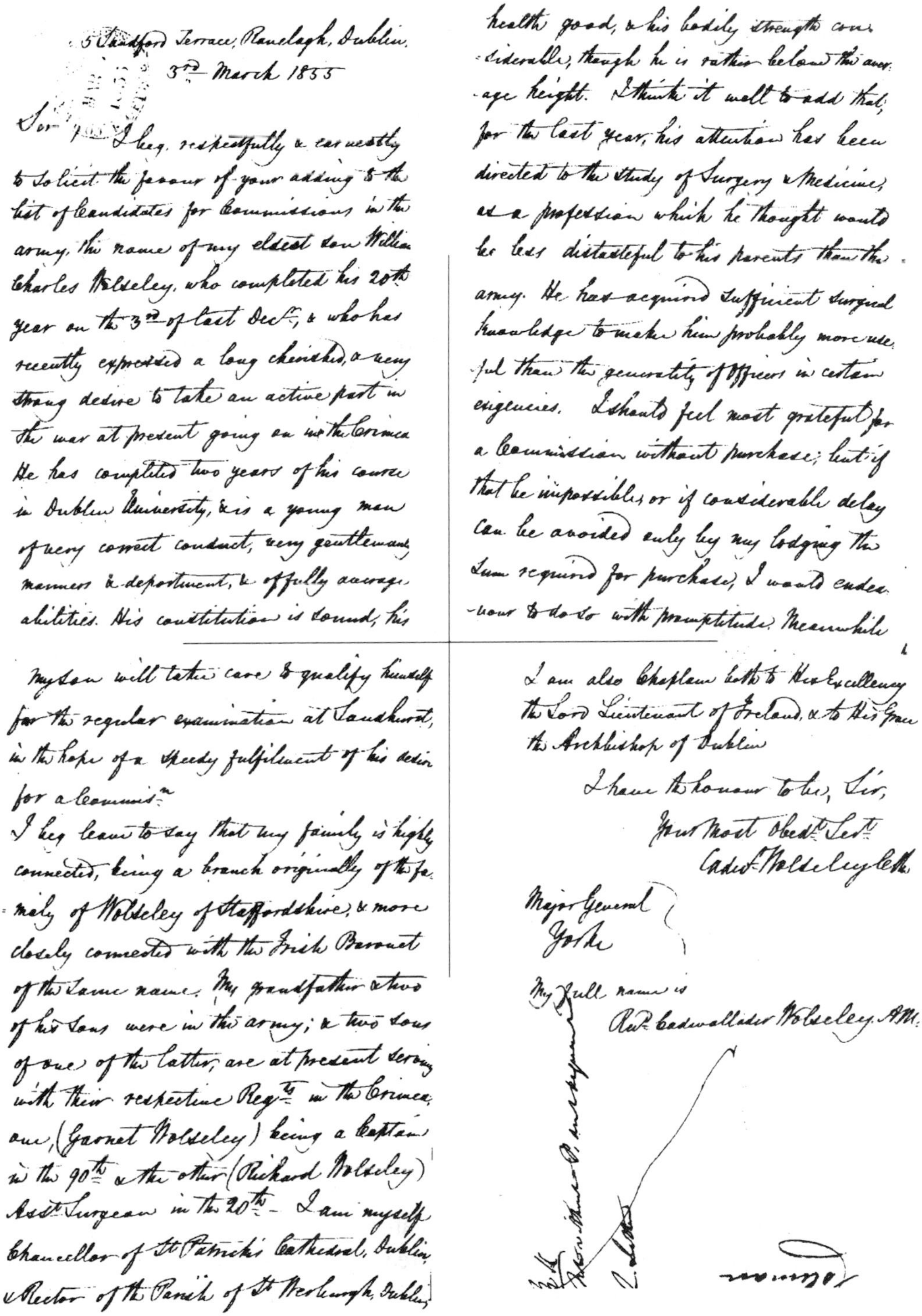

5 Stanford Terrace, Ranelagh, Dublin.
3rd March 1855

Sir,
I beg, respectfully & earnestly
to solicit the favour of your adding to the
list of Candidates for Commissions in the
army, the name of my eldest son William
Charles Wolseley, who completed his 20th
year on the 3rd of last Decr, & who has
recently expressed a long cherished, & very
strong desire to take an active part in
the war at present going on in the Crimea.
He has completed two years of his course
in Dublin University, & is a young man
of very correct conduct, very gentlemanly
manners & deportment, & of fully average
abilities. His constitution is sound, his

myself son will take care to qualify himself
for the regular examination at Sandhurst,
in the hope of a speedy fulfilment of his desire
for a commission.
I beg leave to say that my family is highly
connected, being a branch originally of the family of Wolseley of Staffordshire, & more
closely connected with the Irish Baronet
of the same name. My grandfather & two
of his sons were in the army; & two sons
of one of the latter, are at present serving
with their respective Regts in the Crimea,
one (Garnet Wolseley) being a Captain
in the 90th & the other (Richard Wolseley)
Asst Surgeon in the 20th. I am myself
Chancellor of St Patrick's Cathedral, Dublin
& Rector of the Parish of St Werburgh, Dublin

health good, & his bodily strength con-
-siderable; though he is rather below the aver-
-age height. I think it well to add that,
for the last year, his attention has been
directed to the study of Surgery & Medicine,
as a profession which he thought would
be less distasteful to his parents than the
army. He has acquired sufficient surgical
knowledge to make him probably more use-
-ful than the generality of officers in certain
exigencies. I should feel most grateful for
a Commission without purchase; but if
that be impossible, or if considerable delay
can be avoided only by my lodging the
sum required for purchase, I would endea-
-vour to do so with promptitude. Meanwhile

I am also Chaplain both to His Excellency
the Lord Lieutenant of Ireland, & to His Grace
the Archbishop of Dublin.
I have the honour to be, Sir,
Your most obedt Servt
Cadwr Wolseley Clk.

Major General
Yorke

My full name is
Revd Cadwallader Wolseley. A.M.

Fig 6 Commander-in-Chief's Memoranda - William Charles Wolseley. (WO 31/1078)

Reference	Dates of Compilation	Notes
WO 25/744-748	1809-1810	Arranged alphabetically, they contain details of military service only.
WO 25/749-779	1828	Made by officers who had retired on full or half-pay and refers to service completed before 1828. Arranged alphabetically and gives the age at commission, date of marriage and children's births as well as military service. Related correspondence from officers, whose surnames begin with D to R only, is in WO 25/806-807.
WO 25/780-805	1829	Made by serving officers, these are arranged by regiment and give similar information to the 1828 series. The Army List for 1829 serves as an index to it.
WO 25/808-823	1847	Completed by retired officers and refers to service completed before this date. It is arranged alphabetically and contains the same information as the 1828 series.
WO 25/824-870	1870-1872	Includes a few returns before 1870 and after 1872. It is arranged by year of return and then by regiment.

An incomplete name index to service records in WO 25 is available in the Research Enquiries Room.

3.6.2 Regimental service records

Service records were kept by the regiments only, until the early nineteenth century, when the War Office began to taken an interest. There are two indexes to both the early Regimental and War Office series (WO 76 and WO 25), one an index to regiments, and the other to names. The records of service of officers for the late nineteenth century to 1920 are in WO 339 and WO 374.

Regimental records of officers' services start in 1755. Those for service prior to 1914 are in WO 76, but the records of the Gloucester Regiment, 1792-1866, are in WO 67/24-27, and those of the Royal Garrison Regiment, 1901-1905, are in WO 19. There are also some oddments in WO 25. Artillery officers' services, 1727-1751, are in WO 54/684: for 1771-1870, they are in WO 76. Returns of engineer officers, 1786-1850, are in WO 54/248-259, with service records, 1796-1922, in WO 25/3913-3919. Not all regiments are represented, and the records of some were lost. The information kept by the regiments varies a great deal, but it usually gives the ranks held, service details, and some personal particulars. The WO 76 service record for Major W C Wolseley is described in the case study in section 3.9.2 and also reproduced as **figure** 7. There is an incomplete card index to regimental service records in the Reference Room, Kew. There are many regimental publications of officers' services.

Not all officers were regimental officers. For staff officers, there is a staff pay index, 1792-1830 (WO 25/695-699), lists of staff at various dates between 1802 and 1870, some with addresses (WO 25/700-702) and general returns of staff in British and foreign stations, 1782-1854 (WO 25/703-743). There are general returns of the service of commissariat officers, who were not military officers, for 1798-1842 (WO 61/1-2), followed by a register of Commissariat and Transport staff, 1843-1889 (WO 61/5-6). Senior staff of the War Office are included in the *Army Lists*.

From 1870, individual units would keep details on individual officers on an Army Form B 194-1. A confidential report on each officer was completed yearly by the Commanding Officer of the unit and these were sent to the Military Secretary's Department of the War Office. Very few confidential reports have been preserved. Correspondence files on officers who served between 1870 and 1922 are now in WO 339 and WO 374. WO 339 is arranged by War Office 'Long Number' and the alphabetical index to these numbers is in WO 338, which is seen on microfilm. WO 374 is arranged in alphabetical order. Many files of officers who were commissioned before 1901 have not survived.

3.6.3 Records of service kept by the Military Secretary, 1870-1922

In 1871 it was decided to cease the system of obtaining commissions by purchase. In conjunction with these changes a new system of personal record keeping was begun by the Military Secretary's department of the War Office. From 1870

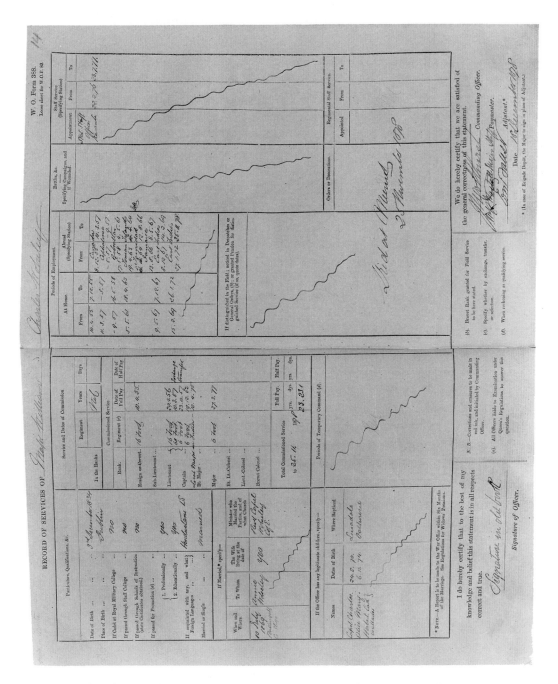

Fig 7 Officer's Service Record - Major W C Wolseley. (WO 76/261, p 14)

individual units would keep details on individual officers on an Army Form B 194-1 and these would in turn be bound into Army Books 83. These records are in WO 76. A confidential report on each officer was completed yearly by the Commanding Officer of the unit and these were kept by the Military Secretary. Very few confidential reports have been preserved.

Together with these two forms was a correspondence file, which, depending on length of service, could become very bulky. These correspondence files, covering service of any officer between 1870 and 1922, are arranged in two separate record classes, WO 339 and WO 374, and contain military correspondence. They can contain details of an officer's estate, should he have died in service, reports made by repatriated prisoners of war, details relating to pensions, medical records, etc.

WO 339 is arranged by War Office 'Long Number' and the alphabetical index providing these numbers can be found in WO 338 (available on microfilm). WO 374 is arranged in alphabetical order. In total some 217,000 individual files can be found in these two classes. Unfortunately many files of officers who obtained their commissions prior to 1901 were destroyed in the 1930's. Files of those officers who saw service after 1922 are still maintained by the Ministry of Defence.

Further details about these records can be found in *Army Service Records of the First World War*, S Fowler, W Spencer and S Tamblin (London, 1997) and in section 16.2.2.

3.6.4 Further information and miscellaneous series

A few papers and correspondence relating to individual officers are in WO 43. Particulars of service and some personal information for a small number of mainly senior officers, 1830-1961, can be found in a series of selected personal files in WO 138. These records are not available for public inspection until *75 years* after the closure of the file. A few confidential reports on officers, 1872-1905, are included in WO 27/489.

Inspection returns in WO 27, for the period 1750 to 1857, record the presence or absence of officers from their regiments at the time of inspection and may contain a brief record of service. The absence of officers is also recorded in the monthly returns, 1759-1865, in WO 17.

Additions to the list of general officers receiving unattached pay, that is, pay other than from their regiment, 1835-1853, are recorded in WO 25/3230-3231. Staff paybooks and returns, 1782-1870, are in WO 25/689-743. Ledgers of the payment of unattached pay, 1814-1896, are in PMG 3. Alphabetical registers of those receiving unattached pay, 1872-1880, are in WO 23/66-67.

A list of officers killed and wounded at the Battle of Waterloo is contained in Wellington's despatch of 29 June 1815, printed as a supplement to the *London Gazette* of 1 July 1815: copies can be found in ZJ 1/138 and MINT 16/111. A list of officers (and men) present during the siege of Fort Mary, Lydenburg, South Africa in 1881 is in WO 32/7820. A list of officers present during the siege of Ladysmith, South Africa in 1899-1900 is in WO 32/7114B.

3.7 Half Pay and Pensions

3.7.1 Half pay

Not until 1871 were officers entitled to a pension on retirement. Before then, officers who wished to retire either sold their commissions, recouping their capital investment, or went on to half pay. The system of half pay was set up in 1641 for officers of reduced or disbanded regiments. In time it became essentially a retaining fee, paid to officers so long as a commission was held; thus they were, in theory if not in practice, available for future service. It might also be paid to officers unfit for service and this was officially sanctioned after 1812. During the nineteenth century the system became more and more heavily abused. Officers who could afford to go onto half pay could avoid service abroad or any unwelcome posting. It was also possible to buy a commission and then go on half pay the next day, which made officers eligible to purchase the next commission up without serving any time with the regiment. Officers receiving half pay are listed in the Army List but do not always appear in the index.

Registers of half pay officers are in WO 23. A series of alphabetical registers of those in receipt of half pay between 1858 and 1894, giving name, rank, regiment, date of commencement, rate and a record of payments, is in WO 23/68-78. These are often annotated with the date of the officer's death.

Ledgers recording the issue of half pay from 1737 to 1921 are in PMG 4. Until 1841 these are arranged by regiment and unindexed; thereafter they are arranged alphabetically by name. Deaths, the assignment of pay, and sales of commissions are noted in the ledgers, and from 1837 they give addresses. Later volumes also give dates of birth.

Lists of those entitled to receive half pay between 1713 and 1809, arranged by regiment, are in WO 24/660-747. WO 25/2979-3002 contain further nominal lists, for the period 1712 to 1763, and registers of warrants for half pay between 1763 and 1856. Replies to a circular of 1854, with details of the fitness for service of half pay officers, may be found in WO 25/3009-3012. Further miscellaneous lists relating to half pay are in WO 25/3003-3008, 3013-3016.

Registers of half pay disbursed to officers living abroad are in WO 25/3017-3019; these cover the period 1815 to 1833. WO 25/3232 is a register of permissions granted to officers on half pay to be abroad between 1815 and 1833.

Claims from wounded officers for half pay between 1812 and 1858 are contained in a series of letterbooks in WO 4/469-493.

3.7.2 Retired full pay

A few officers, mainly those with a letter of service for raising an invalid or a veteran corps, were entitled to retired full pay. Registers of those receiving such pay, 1872-1894, are included in WO 23/66-74. Further registers, 1830-1870, are in WO 25/3000-3004. Ledgers of payments, 1813-1896, are in PMG 3.

Registers of payments made to Army (and Royal Marines) officers in reduced circumstances between 1720 and 1738 are in WO 109/55-87.

3.7.3 Pensions for wounds

A system of pensions for wounded officers was set up in 1812 and was available to officers who were wounded before 1812. Registers of those who received such pensions, between 1812 and 1897, are in WO 23/83-92. Correspondence on claims between 1812 and 1855 is in WO 4/469-493. Other correspondence, 1809-1857, is in WO 43, for which there is a card index in the Research Enquiries Room. Ledgers for these payments, 1814-1920, are in PMG 9 .

3.7.4 Widows' pensions and powers of attorncy

Although officers had no entitlement to a pension, provision was made from 1708 for the payment of pensions to widows of officers killed on active service. From 1818, fifteen annuities were also paid to widows of officers whose annual income did not exceed £30 a year out of a fund created by the will of Colonel John Drouly.

Correspondence relating to widows' pensions, 1764-1816, is in WO 4/1023-1030. These volumes are internally indexed.

There are several series of registers of those receiving widows' pensions and the Drouly Annuities:

Reference	Dates	Notes
WO 24/804-883	1713-1829	-
WO 25/3020-3050	1735-1769	Indexes, 1748-1811, are in WO 25/3120-3123.
PMG 11	1808-1920	Not April 1870 - March 1882 (in PMG 10).
WO 23/105-113	1815-1892	-
PMG 10	1870-1882	Continuation of PMG 11.

In addition, there are several series of application papers for widows' pensions and dependants' allowances:

Reference	Dates	Notes
WO 42	1755-1908	These papers may include proofs of birth, marriage, death and probate.
WO 25/3089-3197	1760 - c 1818	Arranged alphabetically, with abstracts of the applications between 1808 and 1825 in WO 25/3073-3109. There is an index in the Research Enquiries Room.
WO 43	1818-1855	A few applications only.

Provision of an authentic baptismal certificate was mandatory for those in government service: membership of the established church implied loyalty to the crown. As a result there are many baptismal certificates for Army officers in the War Office records. There are two main caches, for 1777-1868 in WO 32/8903-8920 (code 21A) and for 1755-1908 in WO 42. The latter also contains certificates of marriage, birth of children, death and burial (see below). Indexes to both are available in the Research Enquiries Room.

Reports by officers of their marriage, 1830-1882, are in WO 25/3239-3245; some of the marriages date from the early years of the century. The various military registers of births, marriages and deaths include references to officers' families, if they had followed the drum.

Other than this, more information is likely to be found in military records only if the officer died leaving his family in want. From 1708 there was provision for the payment of pensions to the widows of officers killed on active service; from 1720, pensions were also paid to the children and dependent relatives (usually indigent mothers over fifty) in similar cases, out of the Compassionate Fund and the Royal Bounty. These pensions were not an automatic right, and applicants had to prove their need. Application papers for widows' pensions and dependents' allowances, 1755-1908, which can include proofs of birth, marriage, death, and wills, etc, are in WO 42: other such papers, of uncertain date (1760 - c 1818) are in WO 25/3089-3197, arranged alphabetically, with abstracts of applications, 1808-1825, in WO 25/3073-3089. There is an index in the Research Enquiries Room.

There are lists of widows receiving pensions, 1713-1829 (WO 24/804-883), and 1815-1892 (WO 23/88-92). Registers of payments, 1735-1811, are in WO 25/3020-3058, with indexes to pensions for 1748-1811 (WO 25/3120-3123). Similar registers for 1815-1895 are in WO 23/105-123. Ledgers of payments of widows' pensions, 1808-1920, are in PMG 11, but they give little information. Correspondence relating to widows' pensions, 1764-1816, is in WO 4/1023-1030: the volumes are internally indexed, and contain details on many widows. Selected correspondence on widows' pensions is also in WO 43: there is a card index in the Research Enquiries Room.

There are registers of compassionate allowances awarded to dependents, 1773-1812 (WO 25/3124-3125). Registers of those placed on the Compassionate List, 1858-1894, are in WO 23/114-119, with a summary for 1805-1895 in WO 23/120-123. There are also about 2,000 'compassionate papers' for 1812-1813 (WO 25/3110-3114), which are affidavits by the widows and children, in receipt of a compassionate pension, that they received no other government income. They are in rough alphabetical order, and give details of the officer, often the age of the children, and sometimes the name of the guardian, as well as some indication of county or country of residence (they were sworn before local justices). Correspondence relating to the Compassionate Fund, 1803-1860, is in WO 4/521-590. There are ledgers of payments, for 1779-1812 (WO 24/771-803), and for 1812-1915 (PMG 10), but they give little information. Ledgers of pension payments for the widows of foreign officers, 1822-1885, are in PMG 6 and PMG 7. For pensions and compassionate allowances to the widows and dependents of commissariat officers, 1814-1834, see WO 61/96-98.

Registers of pensions to the widows of Royal Artillery and Royal Engineer officers, 1833-1837, are in WO 54/195-196, with ledgers of payments, 1836-1875, in PMG 12. There is also a series of indexed registers of letters of attorney, 1699-1857, relating to Ordnance officers, civilian staff and creditors who expected to receive payments of any kind from the Ordnance Office (WO 54/494-510): many of these letters were made in favour of the wife or other close relative, or were letters granted by the probate courts to the widow as executrix.

Similar registers of powers of attorney for Army officers in general are in PMG 14 and PMG 51. There are entry books of powers of attorney apparently arranged by date, for 1759-1816 (PMG 14/104-125). For 1811-1814, there are alphabetical entry books (PMG 14/126-137). Registers of letters of attorney, 1756-1827, are in PMG 14/142-167: they include separate volumes of letters of attorney granted by widows, 1802-1821 (PMG 165-167). There is a single register of letters of attorney, 1755-1783, at WO 30/1. Later registers, 1836-1899, are in PMG 51.

3.7.5 Children's and dependent relatives' allowances

From 1720 pensions were also paid to children and dependent relatives of officers out of the Compassionate Fund and the Royal Bounty. There are registers of compassionate allowances awarded to dependents, 1773-1812 (WO 25/3124-3125). Registers giving the names of those placed on the Compassionate List, 1858-1894, are in WO 23/114-119, with a summary for 1805-1895 in WO 23/120-123. Applications for grants from the Fund, for 1812 and 1813 only, are in WO 25/3110-3114. Ledgers recording payments for 1779-1812 are in WO 24/771-803 and for 1812-1815 are in PMG 10. Correspondence relating to the Compassionate Fund, 1803-1860, is in WO 4/521-590.

3.8 Recruitment and Training

Little formal training was provided to new recruits, other than those recruited to those branches of the service requiring technical skills, before the nineteenth century. In 1741 the Royal Military Academy was established to train artillery and engineer officers. This was merged in 1947 with the Royal Military College, founded in 1807 and based at Sandhurst since 1812. Sandhurst holds registers of cadets from c 1790 and applications for entry which may include baptism certificates. These records may be consulted by arrangement with the commandant. See also section 14.11.

3.9 Case Studies

These two case studies illustrate how a detailed picture of an individual's service history can be built up using a variety of different sources.

3.9.1 Major General William Freke Williams

This officer was brought to my attention by a friend of many years who had in her possession a privately printed family history, written and produced just after the turn of the century. Written without access to many of the official records of the War Office, was the information in the family history correct?

William Freke Williams was born in 1792. On 30 August 1810, he obtained a commission without purchase as an Ensign in The Royal African Corps (WO 25/60 f 303), signalling the beginning of what was to be a very successful military career.

A Lieutenancy in the Royal African Corps followed on 10 June 1811 (WO 25/61, f 172). During his time in the Royal African Corps, he saw service in Senegal, Goree and Sierra Leone, all on the west coast of Africa. On 26 March 1813 Williams purchased a commission as a Lieutenant in the 85th Foot. Service with the 85th Foot was to take him to the Iberian Peninsula, fighting the French at the battles of San Sebastian, Nivelle and Nive. For his service at these battles, he was awarded the Military General Service Medal with three clasps (WO 100/1).

After service in the Peninsular War, the 85th Foot went to America where Lieutenant Williams was wounded at the battle of Bladenburg on 24 August 1814 (WO 1/141, f 33). He then purchased a Captaincy in the 85th Foot on 31 October 1814 (WO 25/64, f 258).

Subsequent service in the West Indies and Canada brought him to the attention of the Commander in Chief. Promotion to Major in 1825 (WO 25/193, f 28) and being created a Knight of Hanover in 1834/5 were just the next steps in his still rising career. After service in Canada in 1838 he was promoted to Lieutenant Colonel in June of that year. Further special service was to follow. An appointment as Assistant Adjutant General (AAG) in Belfast in 1844 was to last until 1855. During his time as AAG at Belfast, Lieutenant Colonel Williams became Colonel Williams (WO 25/77, f 254).

In 1855, to assist the British forces participating in the Crimean War, Williams was promoted to Brigadier General and given command of a Brigade of some 4000 men on Malta. On 14 April, 1857 he was promoted to Major General and given command of a Brigade at Gibraltar. When the garrison at Gibraltar was reduced he returned to England to command a Brigade at Shorncliffe.

Ill health in the early part of 1860 forced Major General WF Williams reluctantly to resign his command. He died at Bath on 12 December 1860 and is buried in the parish churchyard at Widcombe in Bath.

Much of this record of service was contained in the family history, although certain minor omissions had been made. Apart from missing the information about the Royal African Corps most of the basic facts were present and could be confirmed by the Official Army List, Hart's Army List, War Office Notification Books in WO 25 and Field Officers Records of Service in WO 25/3998-4001. The entry relating to Williams from Hart's Army List is reproduced as **figure 5**.

3.9.2 Major W C Wolseley

The wealth of detail about the career of an officer who died in service can be demonstrated by the case of William Charles Wolseley.

As with looking for any officer from 1757 onwards, the first place to look for an officer is in the Army List (see section 3.2). This will not only provide you with the rank and regiment of an individual, it will also tell you the dates on which the officer obtained a commission at a given rank. It is important when using the Army List to find the first and last entry for an individual, as many officers saw service in more than one regiment.

For any officer who obtained a commission between 1793 and 1870, whether it be by purchase or on merit, the place to begin research, once you have checked the Army List, is WO 31 Commander in Chief (C in C), Memoranda Papers. Before an individual could be granted a commission, the C in C had to sanction it. The papers in WO 31 are arranged in date order and the class list provides the date of the relevant memoranda in the left-hand column of the document description and the date the commission was announced in the *London Gazette*, which is the date in the Army List, in the right-hand column.

Information contained in a C in C's memorandum can vary. If the commission was by purchase, it will record the amount paid, the rank being purchased and the regiment. For commissions granted on merit, the reasons why such a commission should be granted are usually given. First commissions granted to individuals (usually as an Ensign (infantry) or Cornet (cavalry) are usually accompanied by a lengthy letter from a member of his family, or a suitable patron, describing his potential and character and explaining why such a commission is being sought.

The C in C's memoranda for the appointment of William Charles Wolseley as an Ensign into the 16th Foot, dated April 1855, can be found in WO 31/1078. Within the memoranda is a letter dated 3 March 1855 from Reverend Cadwallada Wolseley asking for a commission for his eldest son, William Charles Wolseley - see **figure 6**. The letter describes his attributes; his family, noting a connection with Captain Garnet Wolseley (later Field Marshal Viscount Garnet Wolseley); his physical description; and current place of residence. The letter also provides information about the writer of the letter, noting that he was chaplain to the Lord Lieutenant of Ireland and also to the Archbishop of Dublin.

Charles Wolseley's next two commissions were both by purchase. A Royal Commission in 1821 set the amount which should be paid but these levels were exceeded on numerous occasions. The memoranda for Wolseley's commission as a Captain in the 6th Foot, dated 19 December 1862, are in WO 31/1307. For his Captaincy in the 6th Foot Wolseley paid the sum of £1100, which interestingly is the difference between the sum paid for a Lieutenancy and a Captaincy as set by the Royal Commission back in 1821.

Apart from the records in WO 31 and information contained in the Army List, records of service of army officers can be found in the record class WO 76. A name index for this class is in the Research Enquiries Room. The records of service for the 6th Foot are in WO 76/261, with Wolseley appearing on page 14 (see **figure 7**). This record of service notes the date of his birth, the dates of all of Wolseley's commissions, together with the regiments he served in, service overseas, details of his wife and children and most importantly his date of death at Meerut in India on 25 November 1878.

As a widow of a British Army Officer, Annie Wolseley applied for a pension. Records of widow's pensions can be found in PMG 11, which is arranged in chronological order and alphabetically by name of the deceased. Details of the pension granted to Annie Wolseley can be found in PMG 11/74, which shows that a pension of £68 7s 2d per year was authorized on 2 May 1879.

4

OTHER RANKS, 1660-1913

4.1 Introduction

In the Army, the 'other ranks' were the privates (infantry) and troopers (cavalry), trumpeters and drummers, supervised by corporals and sergeants who were non-commissioned officers (NCOs) promoted from the ranks. Specialist corps and regiments, however, used different names. A basic outline of ranks in the Army is in appendix 2.

Most men enlisted voluntarily and for 'life', in practice for twenty-one years, and served until they were disabled by wounds or old age, although in wartime enlistment for a limited period was sometimes permitted. Discharges could be bought, but few had the money to do so. The Army Enlistment Act 1870 introduced a scheme whereby men could join the Army on a short-service engagement of twelve years, of which six would be spent with the colours and six on reserve. However, men could still re-engage for a maximum service of twenty-one years. Pay was poor and further reduced by stoppages for food and clothing. Before the late eighteenth century, information about 'other ranks' is sparse and largely to be found in accounts or pension records.

To trace the service record of an individual, it is important to know the approximate dates of his service and the regiment or corps he served in. Almost all service records were kept by the individual regiments, not by any central authority. As a result, if you are searching for an individual soldier, you really do need to know the regiment in which he served, unless you are prepared for a lengthy and speculative search. However, there are two series of Army-wide returns of service of non-commissioned officers and men. One contains statements of periods of service and of liability to serve abroad, as on 24 June 1806 (WO 25/871-1120). The other contains returns of the service of non-commissioned officers and men not known to be dead or totally disqualified for service, who had been discharged between 1783 and 1810 (WO 25/1121-1131). Both series are arranged by regiment, and only then alphabetically.

The main everyday service records of men in active service kept by the Army were the regimental muster book and the regimental pay list. These provide a fairly complete guide to a soldier's Army career from enlistment, through movements with the regiment throughout the world, to discharge. However, because there are so many muster books and pay lists, and because they each cover such a short space of time, it can be a very lengthy task to search through them. It is worth investigating other records first, particularly the service records of soldiers retired to pension, where the personal information is consolidated and is far more easily found, even if you are not sure that your ancestor received a pension. If you find that he was discharged without a pension before 1883, you may have to use the muster books and pay lists. If your soldier died in service, you may find out quite a lot of information if you know the regiment, by using the casualty returns: if these prove no use, try the muster books.

4.2 Identifying a Regiment

There is a computerized index recording the names of soldiers who were discharged to pension between 1760 and 1854 whose records are in the record class WO 97 - see section 4.3. It does not include regiments on the Irish establishment before 1822. A supplementary collection of discharge papers covering the period 1843-1899 in WO 97 is not covered by the database.

It may be possible to identify the unit from old photographs. A useful article is D J Barnes, 'Identification and dating: military uniforms' in *Family history in focus*, ed D J Steel and L Taylor (Guildford, 1984). There is also a chapter on the subject in Norman Holding, *More Sources of World War I Army Ancestry* (FFHS, 1991).

The registers of births of children of army personnel held by the General Register Office are indexed and it may be possible to determine a regiment from them, if you have some idea of when children were born or the area where a soldier served. For further details about these registers see section 19.1 and appendix 4.

If you know the county or country in which your ancestor was living between 1842 and 1862 for England or Scotland, or between 1842 and 1882 for Ireland and abroad, you may be able to pinpoint the regiment from the records of payment of pensions in WO 22 and PMG 8, which include the names of regiments in which individuals served. For further details of these records see section 4.7. If the soldier died in service, another possibility would be to check the records of soldiers' effects, which survive between 1810-1822, 1830-1844 and 1862-1881. They are in WO 25, arranged by initial letter of surname, and they give the regiment. This source is unlikely to be of use if the soldier died owing money to the Army.

If you have any idea about the place of service you may be able to identify the regiment from one of the sources listed in section 1.6.

There are other possibilities as well, although using the following suggestions may be a lengthy process. Depending on the known information, an area of records to be searched can be limited. If a rough date of discharge is known, it may be possible to trace the regiment in which a soldier served by using various registers of discharges. These are not complete but, especially before the records in WO 97 are arranged purely alphabetically, they are a useful potential source of information. A number of these pieces contain information on soldiers whose discharge document would not, in any case, be contained in WO 97. These discharges were:

1817-1829	by purchase	WO 25/3845-3847
1830-1838	by own request	WO 25/3848-3849
1830-1856	with modified pension	WO 25/3850
1838-1855	free or free deferred pension	WO 25/3851-3858
1856-1861	free permanent pension	WO 25/3859-3861
1861-1870	free permanent pension, modified/deferred pension, or purchase	WO 25/3863-3868
1852-1870	first period, incorrigible, ignominy, penal servitude, or 21 years with militia	WO 25/3869-3878
1856-1857	regiment under reduction	WO 25/3879-3882
1866-1870	Limited Service Act	WO 25/3883-3893
1863-1878	on return from India	WO 12/13077-13105
1871-1884	general register	WO 121/223-238
1882-1883	Gosport discharge depot musters	WO 16/2284
1883-1888	Gosport discharge depot musters (index in Research Enquiries Room)	WO 16/2888-2916
1884-1887	without pension (gives address to which discharged)	WO 121/239-257

4.3 Service Records

4.3.1 Soldiers' documents

The most important records are attestation and discharge papers, forming the class known as soldiers' documents in WO 97, which cover the period between 1760 and

1913. **Until 1882, these service records are normally only for men who *were discharged and received a pension*. Soldiers' documents for soldiers who died whilst serving, or who did not receive a discharge certificate for any reason, have not survived.** Except for the early years, where the level of detail is limited, the documents give information about age, physical appearance, birthplace and trade or occupation on enlistment in the Army. They also include a record of service, including any decorations awarded, promotions and reductions in rank, crimes and punishments, and the reason for the discharge to pension. In some cases, place of residence after discharge and date of death are given. An example - relating to Private Benjamin Harris - is reproduced as **figure 8** and further described in the case study in section 4.9.1.

These documents are arranged by discharge date. The order in many boxes has been considerably disturbed over the years so that it may mean looking through a whole box to find a particular individual.

The documents fall into four series:

1760-1854 These documents are arranged alphabetically by name within regiments, which is why it is vital to know the regiment in which a soldier served. There seem to be relatively few for men who enlisted before 1792. This series is available on microfilm at Kew and there is a computerized index which records name, regiment, birthplace, age at discharge and years of enlistment and discharge.

1855-1872 These are again arranged alphabetically by name within a regiment, and it is vital to know the regiment in which a man served.

1873-1882 These are arranged alphabetically by name of soldier within the categories - cavalry, artillery, engineers, foot guards, infantry and miscellaneous corps.

1883-1913 This series covers both soldiers discharged to pension and those discharged for other reasons, such as the termination of limited engagements or discharge by purchase. The documents are arranged in surname order. Details of next of kin, wife and children are given.

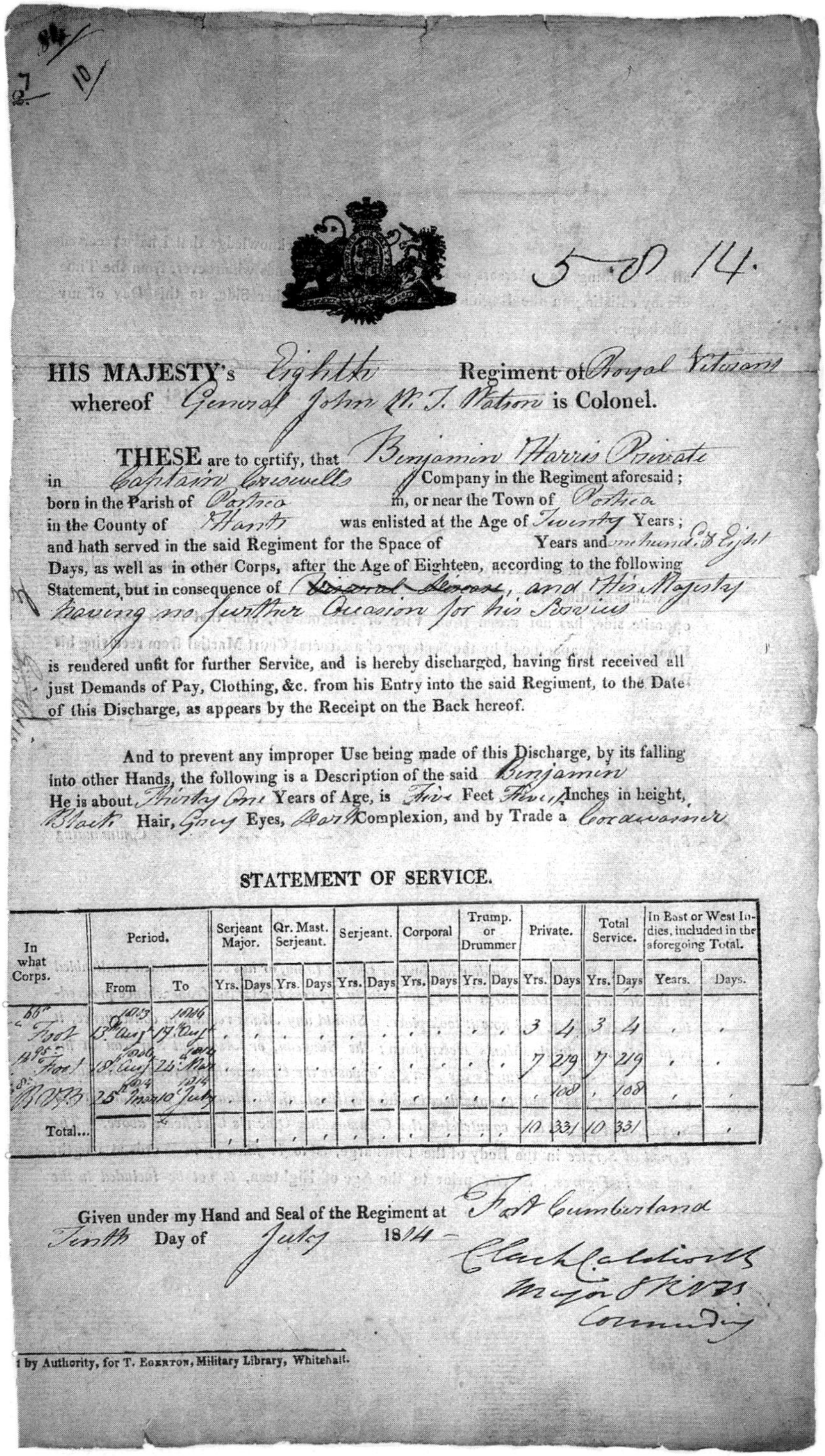

84/
10/

5 O 14.

HIS MAJESTY's Eighth **Regiment of** Royal Veterans **whereof** General John W. T. Watson **is Colonel.**

THESE are to certify, that Benjamin Harris Private in Captain Creswell's Company in the Regiment aforesaid; born in the Parish of Portsea in, or near the Town of Portsea in the County of Hants was enlisted at the Age of Twenty Years; and hath served in the said Regiment for the Space of Years and one hund. & Eight Days, as well as in other Corps, after the Age of Eighteen, according to the following Statement, but in consequence of ~~[illegible]~~, and His Majesty having no further Occasion for his Services is rendered unfit for further Service, and is hereby discharged, having first received all just Demands of Pay, Clothing, &c. from his Entry into the said Regiment, to the Date of this Discharge, as appears by the Receipt on the Back hereof.

And to prevent any improper Use being made of this Discharge, by its falling into other Hands, the following is a Description of the said Benjamin He is about Thirty One Years of Age, is Five Feet Five Inches in height, Black Hair, Grey Eyes, Dark Complexion, and by Trade a Cordwainer

STATEMENT OF SERVICE.

In what Corps.	Period.		Serjeant Major.		Qr. Mast. Serjeant.		Serjeant.		Corporal		Trump. or Drummer		Private.		Total Service.		In East or West Indies, included in the aforegoing Total.	
	From	To	Yrs.	Days	Yrs.	Days	Yrs.	Days	Yrs.	Days	Yrs.	Days	Yrs.	Days	Yrs.	Days	Years.	Days.
66th Foot	13th Aug. 1803	17th Aug. 1806											3	4	3	4		
95th Foot	18th Aug. 1806	24th Mar. 1814											7	219	7	219		
8th R.V.B.	25th Mar. 1814	10th July 1814												108		108		
Total...													10	331	10	331		

Given under my Hand and Seal of the Regiment at Fort Cumberland Tenth Day of July 1814 –

Clark Caldicott
Major 8 R.V.B.
Commanding

[...] by Authority, for T. Egerton, Military Library, Whitehall.

Fig 8 Soldiers' Documents - Private Benjamin Harris. (WO 97/1133)

4.3.2 Additional series of service records

Certificates of service similar to those in WO 97, for men discharged between 1787 and 1813 and awarded Chelsea out-pensions, are in WO 121/1-136. They are arranged in chronological order based on the date of the award of a pension.

General registers of discharges from 1871 to 1884 are in WO 121/223-238. Registers of men discharged without pension between 1884 and 1887 are in WO 121/239-257. Many of the pieces in WO 121 are in very poor condition and access to them may be restricted. Certificates of service of soldiers awarded deferred pensions, 1838-1896, are in WO 131.

Certificates of service for Irish soldiers awarded out-pensions by the Board of Kilmainham Hospital between 1783 and 1822 are in WO 119 (see also section 4.7 below). They are arranged by discharge number, which can be traced in the admission books in WO 118. An example is reproduced as **figure 9**.

4.3.3 Description books

There are two main series of description books. The regimental description and succession books are in WO 25/266-688: covering dates are 1778-1878, but not all the regiments' books start so early or go on so late, and only a small percentage of all soldiers are included. Some are arranged alphabetically, others by date of enlistment. The books give a description of each soldier, his age, place of birth and trade and successive service details. An example is reproduced as **figure 10**. The depot description books, 1768-1908 in WO 67, give the same information, gathered as recruits were assembled at the regimental depot.

These description books in WO 25 are not books containing details of every man in the regiment who served between the covering dates. They began to be compiled in approximately 1825, or slightly earlier, after an investigation into the fraudulent claims of service. Regiments had to write down the services of every man in the regiment who was still serving at that time, and to list them in chronological order of enlistment (or alphabetically). Most books would appear to have between 1,000 and 1,500 names (some have a lot more), but considering that regimental strength was 1,000 and the regiments had been through twenty-two years of war and wastage, this is a small percentage of the total number. Depot rolls or description books (WO 67) are usually much fuller. Men were usually allotted a number, but this number does not appear on any forms until the 1830s. Depot rolls, however, do not list

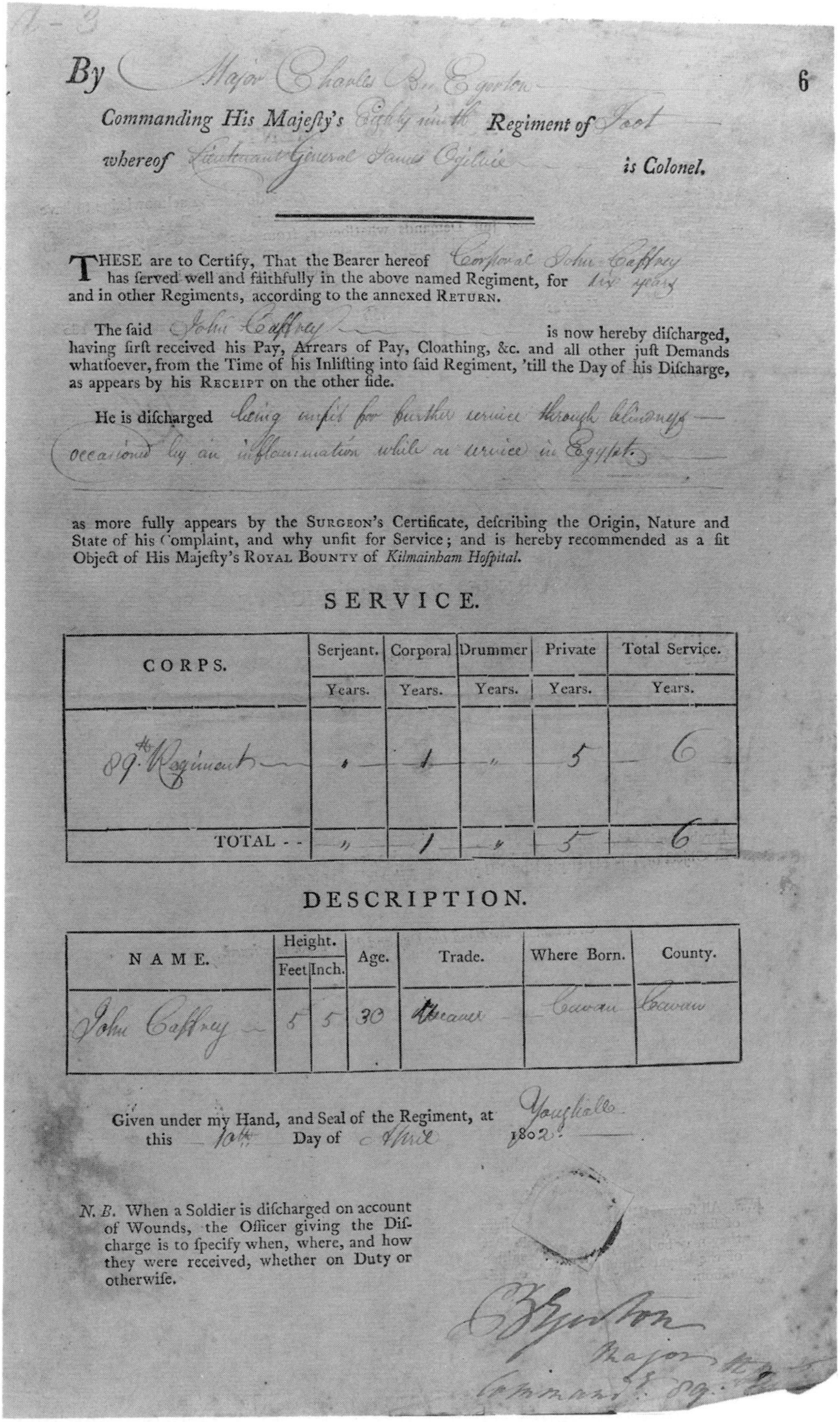

By Major Charles B. Egerton 6

Commanding His Majesty's Eighty ninth Regiment of Foot

whereof Lieutenant General James Ogilvie is Colonel.

THESE are to Certify, That the Bearer hereof Corporal John Caffrey has ſerved well and faithfully in the above named Regiment, for six years and in other Regiments, according to the annexed RETURN.

The ſaid John Caffrey is now hereby diſcharged, having firſt received his Pay, Arrears of Pay, Cloathing, &c. and all other juſt Demands whatſoever, from the Time of his Inliſting into ſaid Regiment, 'till the Day of his Diſcharge, as appears by his RECEIPT on the other ſide.

He is diſcharged being unfit for further service through blindness (occasioned by an inflammation while on service in Egypt)

as more fully appears by the SURGEON'S Certificate, deſcribing the Origin, Nature and State of his Complaint, and why unfit for Service; and is hereby recommended as a fit Object of His Majeſty's ROYAL BOUNTY of *Kilmainham Hoſpital.*

SERVICE.

CORPS.	Serjeant.	Corporal	Drummer	Private	Total Service.
	Years.	Years.	Years.	Years.	Years.
89th Regiment	"	1	"	5	6
TOTAL - -	"	1	"	5	6

DESCRIPTION.

NAME.	Height. Feet	Height. Inch.	Age.	Trade.	Where Born.	County.
John Caffrey	5	5	30	Weaver	Cavan	Cavan

Given under my Hand, and Seal of the Regiment, at Youghall this 10th Day of April 1802.

N. B. When a Soldier is diſcharged on account of Wounds, the Officer giving the Diſcharge is to ſpecify when, where, and how they were received, whether on Duty or otherwiſe.

C B Egerton
Major Comm^d. 89. R^t.

Fig 9 Royal Hospital Kilmainham - Certificate of Service of Corporal John Caffrey. (WO 119/1, f 6)

NAMES.	SIZE. At Enlistment. Feet.	Inches.	At 24 Years of Age. Feet.	Inches.	AGE at Enlistment. Years.	Days.	DESCRIPTION. Complexion.	Eyes.	Hair.	Form of Visage.	Marks, &c.	WHERE BORN. County, City, or Town.	Parish.	TRADE or Occupation.	ATTESTATION, &c. Place.	Date.	For what Period of Service.	By whom enlisted.	FORMER SERVICE — In what Corps, or if on the Out Pension.	Period, deducting Service prior to the Age of 18 Years, and the Time about by Desertion. From.	To.	Actual Service in the East or West Indies, included in the preceding Columns. From.	To.
William Martin	5	9					Fair	Grey	Brown			Lincoln	Baslack	Labourer									
Samuel Mibbit	5	6½			38		Healthy	Hazel	Brown			Lancaster	Ashton	Spinner									
Jno. Carter	5	8			31		Fair	Brown	Brown			Wilts	Town	Blacksmith									
Benjamin Harris	5	5½			31		Dark	Grey	Black	Long		Herts	Portea	Labouring Servant	Winchester	18th Aug 1796	Limited						
Patrick Ryan	5	7			60							Tipperary	Coolitte	Labourer		9th May 1798	Unlimited						
John Sly	5	7½			38							Somerset	Berrow	Miner		9th May 1798	Unlimited						
Richard Hoyate	5	6½			48							Killarney	Mays	Baker		6th Sep 1799	Unlimited						
Thos. Shepherd	5	9½			31		Fresh	Grey	Dark	Long		Kent	Selling	Labourer		26th Sep 1799	Unlimited						
John Nicholson	5	8			41		Fresh	Grey	Brown	Long		Lancaster	Lancaster	Carpenter									
Thomas Stone	5	6½			38		Fair	Grey	Brown	Short		Leicester	Woland	Labourer									

Fig 10 Description Book - Private Benjamin Harris. (WO 25/608)

soldiers who enlisted where the regiment was stationed. Neither do they list soldiers who transferred from one regiment straight into another.

Regimental numbering began as a direct result of this commission of inquiry into fraudulent claims of service. Each man, as he joined, was allotted a consecutive number. This would not be carried throughout his career: if he transferred into another regiment, he would be allotted a new number. It is possible to estimate when a soldier enlisted in a particular regiment if a point of reference is known, ie if a muster provides details of a man with a regimental number close to that of the ancestor. It is then possible to guess a year of discharge (add 21!). In 1917 the system changed and the first series of Army numbers came in. This was very short-lived and the second series (superseding the first) came in in 1922. This allotted 'blocks' of numbers to particular regiments, and a man on first enlistment would be given a number in the relevant block which he would retain even on transfer to another regiment. This numbering system ran out in c 1941 and another began.

4.4 Pay Lists and Muster Rolls

When the regiment in which a soldier served is known or has been ascertained from other records, the muster rolls and pay lists provide a comprehensive means of establishing his date of enlistment, his movements throughout the world and his date of discharge or death. Most of these records cover the period 1760-1898, although those for the artillery go back to 1708. The quarterly muster rolls normally contain three monthly musters and note where the regiment or unit was located; names of officers and men on the strength and their rank, pay, enlistment date (or death or discharge), punishments, time spent in hospital and other absences. The entry may show a man's age on enlistment, as well as the place where he enlisted and, under 'men becoming non-effective',(sometimes found at the end of each quarter's muster), the birthplace, trade and date of enlistment of any soldier discharged or dying during the quarter. From about 1868 to about 1883, at the end of each muster (or at the beginning for regiments stationed in India), may be found a marriage roll, which lists wives and children for whom married quarters were provided. An example of a muster roll from WO 12 is reproduced as **figure 11** and is further described in the case study in section 4.9.2. An example of a Royal Artillery muster roll from WO 10 is reproduced as **figure 15** - see also section 5.3.

The main series of muster books and pay lists are arranged by regiment and are bound in volumes covering a period of twelve months. They are in the following separate classes for:

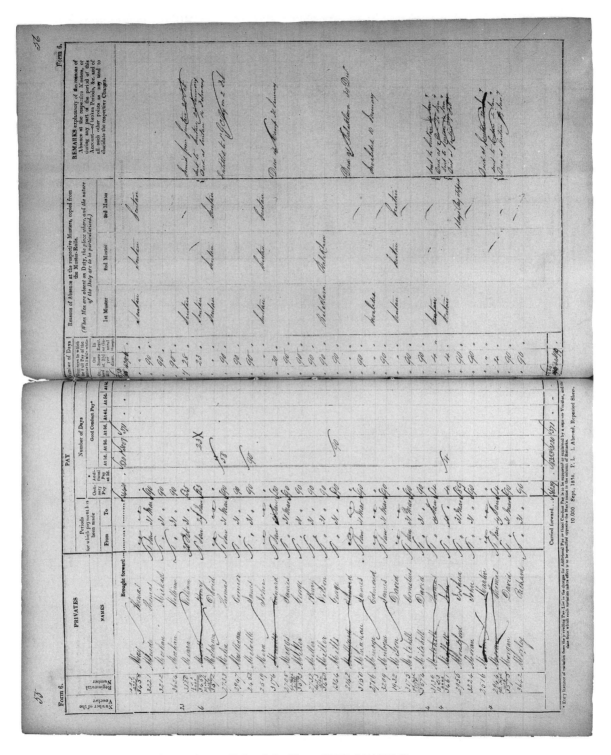

Fig 11 Muster Roll - Private John Moffatt. (WO 12/6519)

Unit	Dates	Class reference
Artillery	1708-1878	WO 10
Engineers	1816-1878	WO 11
General	1732-1878	WO 12
Foreign Legions	1854-1856	WO 15
Scutari Depot	1854-1856	WO 14
Militia and Volunteers	1780-1878	WO 13
All regiments and corps	1878-1898	WO 16

WO 12 includes household troops, cavalry, Guards, regular infantry, special regiments and corps, colonial troops, various foreign legions and regiments, and regimental, brigade and other depots. WO 14 and WO 15 relate to troops engaged in the Crimean War.

WO 16 continues the material in classes WO 10 to WO 12, from 1888 as company muster rolls only, arranged chiefly by regimental districts. From 1882 arrangement of the musters in this class reflects the reorganization of the Army on a territorial basis. The Army Lists contain indexes to regiments with their regimental district numbers.

4.5 Deserters

Desertion was common, as army life was hard and discipline severe. Registers of deserters, 1811-1852, are in WO 25/2906-2934. Until 1827 these volumes consist of separate series for cavalry, infantry and militia (the latter up to 1820 only). After 1827 they are arranged in one series by regiment. They give descriptions, dates and places of enlistments and desertions, and may indicate what happened to deserters who were caught. An example, from WO 25/2925, relating to Private Thomas Brown of the 30th Regiment of Foot, records that he deserted in London on 5 January 1844, having only joined up at the end of the previous December. He was then 17 $\frac{1}{2}$ years old and is described as being 5 feet 6 $\frac{1}{8}$ inches tall, with fresh complexion, brown hair and hazel eyes.

Registers of captured deserters, 1813-1848, with indexes to 1833, are in WO 25/ 2935-2954. They include registers of deserters who were caught or who surrendered, and give the name of the individual and his regiment; the date of his committal and place of confinement; what happened to him (that is, whether he returned to his regiment or was discharged from the Army); and the amount of the reward paid (if the man had not surrendered) and to whom it was paid.

Returns of deserters captured and held as prisoners on the Savoy Hulks, in the Thames Estuary, 1799-1823, are in WO 25/2956-2961. These returns are not indexed. Deserters who surrendered under proclamation between 1803 and 1815 are in WO 25/2955.

Casualty returns in WO 25/1359-2410, 3251-3260, indexed in WO 25/2411-2755, 3261-3471, list deserters as well as casualties for 1809 - c 1875 (the indexes contain some entries up to 1910). Miscellaneous correspondence relating to individual deserters, 1744-1813 and 1848-1858, is in WO 4/591-654.

The *Police Gazette* included in each issue a current list of men who had deserted from the Army (and Royal Marines), with a detailed description of each individual. Copies between 1828 and 1845 are in HO 75. Local newspapers may also carry descriptions of deserters.

Information about deserters, 1716-1830, can also be found in the deserter bounty certificates which are included in numerous other different types of accounts in E 182. These certificates record the payment of rewards to the captors of deserters and there is an incomplete card index by surname of deserter.

A list of deserters at large in Australia has been published in Yvonne Fitzmaurice, *Army deserters from HM Service* (vol 1, Forest Hill, Vic, 1988). A copy of this book is available at Kew.

4.6 Women in the Army

Until women nurses were first recruited during the Crimean War (see section 14.7), no woman formally served in the British Army. One or two, however, did enlist pretending to be men, although there are no separate records for these women. Six wives of soldiers in each company were carried on strength to act as unofficial cooks, laundresses and servants to officers. In addition, there were a large number of camp followers who, unlike the army wives, were not entitled to an issue of 'the King's victuals'. Little is known about these women.

There are very few records of these people. Wives of soldiers are recorded in the soldiers' discharge documents, in WO 97, from the 1850s onwards. Occasionally women retained on strength may appear in the muster rolls in WO 12 and WO 16 under the 'Married Establishment'.

4.7 Pension Records

4.7.1 Administration of pensions

Before the late seventeenth century there was little provision for disabled soldiers, although they might sometimes be licensed to beg. Petitions from disabled soldiers for relief or places in almshouses may be found with the State Papers. SO 5/310 records such petitions for 1660-1750, with 1784-1898 being found in HO 56, with warrant books for appointments 1750-1960 in HO 118. Formal provision was first made in the late seventeenth century and from 1686 pensions were to be paid to "all non-commission officers and soldiers that are or shall be disabled by wounds in fight or other accidents in the service of the Crown … also … to all such non-commission officers and soldiers as having served the Crown 20 years are or shall become unfit for service". It was financed by a levy on the sale of commissions and an annual deduction of one day's pay from the wages of every soldier in the Army.

Pensions were provided in the form of accommodation for disabled soldiers in the Royal Hospital Chelsea, which was opened in 1692. Most army pensioners (other than officers) eventually became known as Chelsea Pensioners, whether they lived in the Royal Hospital or not. Soldiers on the Irish establishment were accommodated at the Royal Hospital Kilmainham, established in 1679 and opened in 1684. These pensions became known as in-pensions.

Within a few months the accommodation became insufficient to meet the demand, and a system of out-pensions for non-residents was devised to supplement the original in-pensions. They could be claimed on the grounds of disability or unfitness arising from service. In the 1750s regulations were passed to make length of service and character the principal reasons for award of pensions, and not disability. Responsibility for the out-pensions of Irish pensioners passed to Chelsea in 1822, and for in-pensioners in 1929.

Except for a few officers admitted as in-pensioners, the two hospitals were not concerned with officers' pensions. The Board of Ordnance was responsible for paying pensions to its own troops until 1833.

The major series of records created as a result were the Soldiers' Documents (WO 97) described in section 4.3. Additional information can be found in many further series.

For a brief account of both the Royal Hospitals see the PRO *Guide* Part 1, section 704/6/3.

4.7.2 Out-pensions

Out-pensioners were formed into Invalid, Veteran and Garrison companies for garrison duties in wartime and in the nineteenth century were often sent out to colonies as settlers - see sections 4.8 and 14.5.

There are three main series of records containing information about out-pensioners: admission books, regimental registers and pension returns. These series cover the vast majority of pensioners at home and abroad.

4.7.3 Admission books

These are arranged chronologically by date of examination for the award of an out-pension, and are not indexed. Therefore you need to know at least the approximate date of a man's discharge from the army and his application for a pension before a search becomes practicable. For 1806-1838, there is a name index in WO 120.

For pensions awarded by the Royal Hospital Chelsea, there are two series of admission books covering pensions awarded for disability, 1715-1913, in WO 116/1-124, 186-251. Details of pensions awarded for length of service, 1823-1913, are in WO 117. For pensions awarded by the Royal Hospital Kilmainham between 1704 and 1922 there is just one series in WO 118. An example of a page from a WO 116 admission book is reproduced as **figure 12**.

Each book gives the date of examination; a brief record of service; the reason why a pension was awarded; place of birth; and a physical description. Between 1830 and 1844 the Chelsea admission books are duplicated by registers in WO 23/1-16, where in addition the intended place of residence is given. The registers, 1838-1844, in WO 23/10-16 are indexed.

4.7.4 Regimental registers

Each regiment kept registers of men who were discharged to pension and these are in two distinct series in WO 120. The first, 1715-1843, in WO 120/1-51 is arranged chronologically within regiments, and gives date of admission, age, a brief record of service, rate of pension, 'complaint', place of birth and a physical description. The volumes for 1839 to 1843 are indexed. In addition, a name index to some infantry

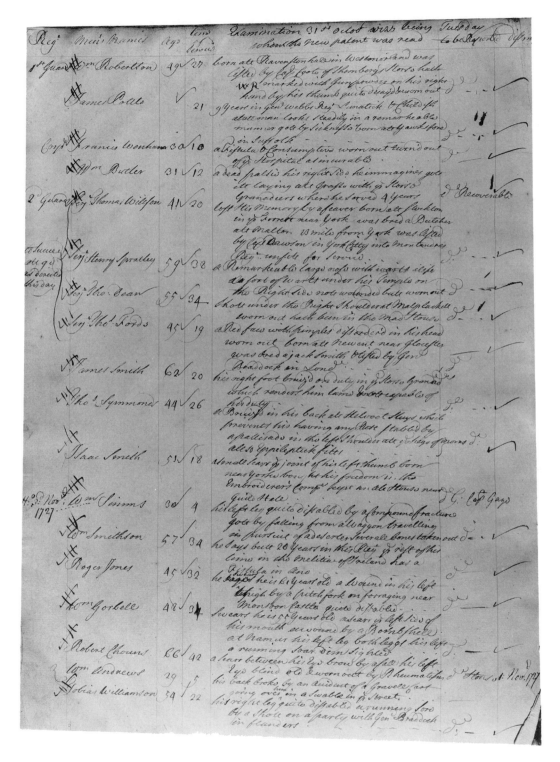

Fig 12 Chelsea Royal Hospital Admission Book, 31 October 1729. (WO 116/2)

regiments, 1806-1858, in WO 120/23-26, 29-30 is kept at Kew. WO 23/20-30 is indexed by J D Beckett, *An index to the regimental registers of the Royal Hospital Chelsea 1806-1838* (Manchester and Lancashire FHS, 1993).

The second series in WO 120/52-70 records pensions being paid between 1814 and 1857. Admissions before 1845 are arranged by rate of pension, those between 1845 and 1857 chronologically. The registers give rate of pension, date of admission and residence, and are marked up with the place of payment of the pension and date of death. These registers are duplicated and extended to 1876 in WO 23/26-65. A similar series of registers of pensions being paid from 1806 to 1807 is in WO 23/136-140.

4.7.5 Pension returns

Before 1842 out-pensions were paid by convenient local officials, such as excise officials. In 1842 payment was made the responsibility of staff officers of pensioners, in a number of districts. Each staff officer made a monthly return to the War Office in which he recorded pensioners who had moved into, or out of, his district, whose pension had ceased, or who had died. Pension returns in WO 22 record pensions paid or payable from district offices between 1842 and 1883. There were about one hundred districts in Great Britain and Ireland.

These returns, which are arranged by district, give the pensioner's name, regiment, rate of pension, date of admission to pension, rank, and the district to which, or from which, he had moved. Also included with the returns are various items of statistical information. Returns for British payment districts cease in 1862, but returns relating to pensions paid overseas and in the colonies extend into the 1880s.

4.7.6 In-pensions

There are muster rolls for in-pensioners of Chelsea Hospital (the men commonly called Chelsea Pensioners) for 1702-1789 in WO 23/124-131, and for 1864-1865 in WO 23/132; a list of in-pensioners, 1794-1816, in WO 23/134; and an alphabetical register, 1837-1872, in WO 23/146.

Admission books for the years 1778-1756 and 1824-1917 are in WO 23/133, 163-172, 174-180. Arranged chronologically, these books give regiment, name, age, service, rate of pension, cause of discharge, date of admission to pension, and decision of the Board of Chelsea Hospital. In addition, an address is often given. An index of in-pensioners admitted between 1858 and 1933 is in WO 23/173.

A list of in-pensioners at the Royal Hospital Kilmainham between 1839 and 1922 is in WO 118/47-48. This list also includes out-pensioners.

4.7.7 Pensions: other sources

Additional information about both in- and out- pensioners at Chelsea can sometimes be found in the Board Minutes and Papers, 1784-1953, in WO 250 and the Invaliding Board Minutes and Papers, 1800-1915, in WO 180, especially where appeals were made against decisions on eligibility for a pension and the rate at which it was to be paid. Minute books in WO 180/53-76 include appeals as well as other relevant papers. The books are incomplete, and date from between 1823 and 1915.

A nominal list of out-pensioners discharged between 1821 and 1829, who had served in the tropics, for which an additional pension was payable, is in WO 23/25.

Some 5000 personal files of soldiers (and sailors) who received a disability pension and who left the armed services before 1914 are in PIN 71. A number of papers for widows' pensions are also included in this class. The files contain medical records, accounts of how and where illness or injuries occurred and men's own accounts of incidents in which they were involved. Conduct sheets are included, recording the place of birth, age, names of parents and family, religion, physical attributes and marital status. These records are arranged alphabetically.

4.7.8 Widows' pensions

Pensions to widows, children and other dependents of non-commissioned officers and men killed on active service have only been paid by the state since 1901. Before then such pensions might be provided by private subscriptions or the Royal Patriotic Fund. Annual reports of the Royal Patriotic Fund, printed with the Parliamentary papers, list the names of widows to whom grants were paid.

4.8 Soldiers Settling Abroad

Pensions were also paid to former British soldiers who had emigrated to the colonies. Chelsea Hospital out-pension registers, 1814-1857, for these men are in WO 120/69-70. Another register, 1845-1854, is in WO 23/31.

Lists of men who emigrated to Australia and New Zealand between 1830 and 1848 under schemes to settle soldiers there are in WO 43/542 (for Australia) and WO 43/853 (New Zealand).

A more detailed description of the sources available is in Stella Colwell, *Family Roots* (London, 1991).

4.9 Case Studies

4.9.1 Private Benjamin Randell Harris of the 66th Foot, 95th Foot and 8th Royal Veterans

As an enlisted man Benjamin Harris was unusual in that in 1848, some thirty-four years after he left the army, his memoirs were published as *Recollections of Rifleman Harris*. This has recently been reprinted as *A Dorset Rifleman: the Recollections of Benjamin Harris*, edited by Eileen Hathaway (Shinglepicker, 1996).

The basic facts of Harris's career recounted in his memoirs are verified by his record of service in WO 97/1133. The records of service of men discharged to pension between 1760 and 1854 are available on microfilm, with an index available on computer. The index can be searched by surname, forename or initial, regiment and place of birth. Although Benjamin Harris might appear to be a common name, only one man with that name who served in the 95th Foot was found amongst the records in WO 97. His attestation form is reproduced as **figure 8**.

Searching on the surname Harris produces 901 entries, but adding in the forename Benjamin reduces this to eight, only one of whom served in the 95th Foot. The computer screen entry looks like this

Surname	Forename	Birthplace	Count(r)y	Enlist Year	Dischge Year	Age
Harris	Benjamin	Portsea	Hampshire	1803	1814	31

Service years	Service months	Regiment	Letter Class Pce	Notes
		F 66 F 95 RV 8	WO 97/ 1133	

This shows that he served in the 66th Regiment of Foot, the 95th Regiment of Foot and the 8th Royal Veteran Battalion.

Although details relating to the career of an individual can be obtained by using other sources, only the records of soldiers discharged to pension at Chelsea Hospital can be found in WO 97. By using the computerized name index to WO 97 it is possible find the records of over 250,000 men discharged between 1760 and 1854.

The description book in WO 25/608 provides a physical description of the man and is reproduced as **figure 10**.

Not mentioned in Harris's memoirs is the medal he was awarded for service in the campaign in Portugal and Northern Spain in 1808-1809. The Military General Service Medal (MGS) was not authorized until 1847 and could only be issued to survivors of campaigns fought between 1793 and 1814. Consequently as Harris's memoirs were not published until 1848 he was alive when the medal was authorized. Private Benjamin Harris 95th Foot was awarded an MGS with clasps for Rolica, Vimiero and Corunna (WO 100/8).

The career of Benjamin Harris is typical of many of the period. It is possible to find out about many men who served in the British Army in the late eighteenth and early nineteenth centuries.

4.9.2 Death in service: Crimean War 1854-1856: Private John Moffatt of the 55th Foot

The majority of deaths which occurred during the Crimean War were as a result of disease rather than as a result of enemy action. The major consequence of the death in service of another rank was the destruction of his record of service. As widows' pensions for other ranks did not become common until the Boer War period (1899-1902), once a soldier's estate had been settled the War Office had no need to keep the record of service as no further money would have be due to any individual.

The records in WO 97 are arranged in chronological batches, but as John Moffatt died in service his record will not be preserved in this class. The most important record classes to use in the case of someone who died in service are the Regimental Musters and Pay Lists in WO 10 - WO 16, the casualty returns in WO 25 and the deaths and effects papers, also in WO 25.

As men who saw active service in the Crimean War, a useful place to start gathering information about a individual soldier is the Crimean War medal roll in WO 100. The medal roll for the Crimean War medal awarded to members of the 55th Foot is in WO 100/30. Private John Moffatt appears on folio 404 for his medal and clasps for the battles at Alma and Inkerman and folio 468 for his clasp for operations at Sebastopol. It is the second entry which notes that he was dead at the time that the medal roll was compiled.

As no record of service for John Moffatt survives, it is necessary to create a picture of his career by using other sources.

Description books (by regiment) of soldiers can be found in WO 25. However there is no surviving book for the 55th Foot.

The muster and pay lists mentioned above (WO 10 - WO 16), are quarterly accounts completed by the regiment which account for all of the manpower in the regiment over a given three month period. The muster will tell you where the muster was taken, who was serving with the regiment (both officers and men), what each soldier was being paid, when an individual left a regiment by whatever cause and if an individual remitted his pay, to whom the money was sent. The musters can also tell you where a regiment travelled during the reporting quarter.

As we know that John Moffatt was alive on 4 November 1855, the date of the Battle of Inkerman, the muster that covers this date can be used as starting point. By working backwards and forwards from this date it is possible to find out when John Moffatt died and when he joined the army.

According to the muster for the period October to December 1854 (WO 12/6518), the 55th Foot were in the Crimea and serving at various locations and John Moffatt was still alive and serving with the regiment. The next muster, for the period January to March 1855 - illustrated as **figure 11** (WO 12/6519), shows that John Moffatt was sent to hospital at Scutari on 4 January and it was there that he died on 7 February 1855. This information is confirmed in the Scutari Depot Muster in WO 14/2.

Working backwards, chronologically through the musters, it is recorded that John Moffatt transferred into the 55th Foot, from the 13th Light Infantry (13 LI), at Gibraltar on 26 March 1854 (WO 12/6517). The muster of this regiment for March 1854 (WO 12/3071) confirms the transfer of John Moffatt, along with a number of other men into various regiments, all heading for the Crimea. Tracing back, muster by muster, the entry of John Moffatt into the 13th Light Infantry was eventually discovered in a muster for the period January to March 1848 (WO 12/3065). He had enlisted in Belfast on 26 January 1848. His height is given but there is no further description of the man. All that the records tell you is when and where he joined, how tall he was, where he served and when he died.

4.9.3 Service in a famous regiment: Colour Sergeant John Harding of the 2/24th Foot

The 24th Foot is one of the best known infantry regiments of the Victorian Army. The annihilation of over 800 British troops, mostly members of the 1/24th and 2/24th Foot (ie the first and second battalions of the regiment), at the Battle of Isandhlwana on 22 January 1879, and the defence at Rorke's Drift by men of the same units on 22/23 January 1879, both actions during the Zulu War, have caused much heartache for researchers who believed their man was there.

John Harding was born in February, 1859 at Hillingdon, near Uxbridge in Middlesex, and enlisted into the 25th Brigade of the army at London on 27 February 1877. He was sent to the 24th Foot depot at Brecon in Wales where he became 25B/1323 Private J Harding, 2/24th Foot.

When the regiment went to South Africa in February 1878, John Harding went with them. By the time of the Zulu War in 1879, John Harding had been promoted to Corporal. When the British Army invaded Zululand in January 1879, they did so in three columns. Men from the 1/24th and 2/24th were dispersed around all three columns. It was men of the 3rd column who fought at the Battle of Isandhlwana and defended Rorke's Drift. John Harding and 'H' company in which he served were in the column commanded by Lord Chelmsford and did not therefore see action at either Isandhlwana or Rorke's Drift. Chelmsford's column arrived at Rorke's Drift on the morning of 23 January. On this particular day John Harding was promoted to Lance Sergeant whilst at Rorke's Drift. (Regimental Order Book South Wales Borderers Museum O 1948 2 refers).

For a detailed study of the action at Isandhlwana and the defence of Rorke's Drift which lists those present at both actions, see *The Silver Wreath: Being the 24th Regiment at Isandhlwana and Rorke's Drift, 1879*, by Norman Holme (Samson Books, 1979).

For his service in the Zulu War, John Harding was awarded the South African War Medal with the clasp 1877-9. Details of all the South African War Medals awarded to the 24th Foot can be found in WO 100/46. **Figure 17** shows the entries for the award of this medal to Private Frederick Hitch and Alfred Henry Hook, both of whom were also awarded the Victoria Cross for their gallantry at Rorke's Drift. The Register of Victoria Cross Awards, illustrated as **figure 16**, gives the reasons for their awards.

After the Zulu War ended, John Harding went on to see over fifteen years service in India. After promotion to Sergeant and then Colour Sergeant, he eventually rose to the rank of Regimental Sergeant Major (RSM). It obviously did suit him, for within three months of his promotion he reverted to Colour Sergeant at his own request. This change of rank was to be the beginning of a sad decline for a man who thus far had had a successful army career.

On 5 June 1891 Colour Sergeant John Harding was tried by regimental court martial for being drunk on duty. He was found guilty and reduced to the rank of Corporal. Soon after the court martial Harding transferred into the 2nd Battalion of the Derbyshire Regiment. Alcoholism continued to plague his career until he was finally discharged from the army at Calcutta on 22 March 1898.

Such is the picture of one man's military career that can be reconstructed from one record; Harding's record of service is in WO 97/2977.

4.9.4 Service in the Boer War 1899-1902: Private Alexander Lee Stanton of the Imperial Yeomanry

Since the advent of the camera, images of soldiers have always very popular. Many soldiers about to travel overseas had their photograph taken so that they could be given to their next of kin. Many of these photographs can provide useful information for the genealogist. It is most unusual for such photographs to survive with the public records. The portrait of Private Stanton, an enlarged detail from a photograph of the first contingent of men of the 42nd (Hertfordshire) Company Imperial Yeomanry (COPY 1/446), reproduced as **figure 13**, is exceptional and is only with the public records because it was registered for copyright protection purposes. The Imperial Yeomanry was formed in late 1899 as a result of the need for mounted infantry in South Africa. and was recruited specifically for service overseas.

Fig 13 Private A L Stanton. (COPY 1/446)

Alexander L Stanton joined the 42nd Company (Hertfordshire) Imperial Yeomanry on 22nd January 1900. He appears to have been unemployed when he joined up. As service in the Imperial Yeomanry was only for one year, Stanton may have enlisted just to see if he liked army life.

After forty days training in England, Stanton, together with the first contingent of 42 Company Imperial Yeomanry left for South Africa. According to his attestation papers, illustrated as **figure 14** (WO 128/20), he had been promoted to corporal by November 1900, when he was discharged from the Imperial Yeomanry to join the Commander in Chief's (C in C's) Bodyguard and he died of wounds received in action on 3 January 1901. As this occurred after he had left the Imperial Yeomanry, it appears that his original unit may have been the only one to retain his records. Attestation papers of the Imperial Yeomanry are available in the record class WO 128 and are arranged in service number order, with the registers in WO 129, see also section 12.4.

The Commander in Chief's Bodyguard was a unit raised in South Africa. Enrolment papers for South African local forces are in the class WO 126 and are arranged alphabetically by name of unit and then alphabetically by name of soldier. The nominal rolls for the South African local forces are arranged as above and are in the class WO 127. The enrolment papers for the C in C's Bodyguard are in WO 126/31-34, with Stanton's papers being in WO 126/34. The enrolment paper for Stanton is very brief but records that he joined the Bodyguard on 20 November, 1900, aged 30, and that he was a scout and that he died. It is interesting to note a variation of next of kin details on the two attestation forms. On the Imperial Yeomanry attestation paper, Stanton's next of kin is given as his mother in Belfast. On the C in C's Bodyguard application paper, Stanton's next of kin is given as his sister in New York.

Men who saw service in the Boer War 1899-1902 were entitled to the Queen's South Africa Medal (QSA). The medal roll for the QSA for the 42nd company Imperial Yeomanry is in WO 100/125. The roll notes that Alexander Stanton was entitled to the medal with the Cape Colony, Transvaal and Wittebergen clasps. The roll also note that he died in South Africa and that he had served in the Commander in Chief's Bodyguard. The QSA medal roll for the C in C's Bodyguard is in WO 100/243. This roll confirms the medal entitlement and that Stanton was a corporal in that unit, with the service number 27469. It also notes his date of death as 3 January 1901, of wounds received in action near Lindley. This date does not tally exactly with the South African Field Force Casualty roll 1899-1902 (WO 108/360), which notes that Stanton died on 6 January 1901, of wounds received three days before. A copy of this roll is available as a printed work in the Microfilm Reading Room.

H-W-V 80,000 1200 Forms
8-5847   B. 111
1

Army Form B. 111.

SHORT SERVICE.

(One year with the Colours.)

ATTESTATION OF

No. *5899*   Name *Alexander L Stanton*   Corps *Imperial Yeomanry*

Questions to be put to the Recruit before Enlistment.

1. What is your Name? ....   1. *Alexander L. Stanton*

2. In or near what Parish or Town were you born? .... {   2. In the Parish of *Potten Bar* in or near the Town of *Barnet* in the County of *Hertfordshire*

3. Are you a British Subject? ....   3. *Yes*

4. What is your Age? ....   4. *27* Years *3* Months.

5. What is your Trade or Calling? ....   5. *None*

6. Have you resided out of your Father's house for three years continuously in the same place, or occupied a house or land of the yearly value of £10 for one year, and paid rates for the same, and, in either case, if so, state where?   6. *Yes*

You are hereby warned that if after enlistment it is found that you have given a wilfully false answer to any of the following seven questions, you will be liable to a punishment of two years' imprisonment with hard labour.

7. Are you, or have you been, an Apprentice? if so, where? to whom? and for what period? }   7. *No*

8. Are you Married? }   8. *No*

9. Have you ever been sentenced to Imprisonment by the Civil Power? }   9. *No*

10. Do you now belong to Her Majesty's Army, the Marines, the Militia, the Militia Reserve, the Royal Navy, the Volunteers, the Yeomanry, the Army Reserve, or the Naval Reserve Force? If so, to what Corps? }   10. *No*

11. Have you ever served in Her Majesty's Army, the Marines, the Militia, the Militia Reserve, or the Royal Navy? If so, state which and cause of discharge }   11. *No*

12. Have you truly stated the whole, if any, of your previous Service? }   12. *Yes*

13. Have you ever been rejected as unfit for Her Majesty's Service? If so, on what grounds? }   13. *No*

14. Are you willing to be vaccinated or re-vaccinated? ....   14. *Yes*

15. For what Corps are you willing to be enlisted, or are you willing to be enlisted for General Service? }   15. *Imperial Yeomanry*

16. Did you receive a Notice, and do you understand its meaning, and who gave it to you? ....   16. *Yes* { Name *W A Hownsssm* Corps *Herts Imp. Cav.*

17. Are you willing to serve upon the following conditions provided Her Majesty should so long require your services?

(a) For a term of one year, unless the War in South Africa lasts longer than one year, in which case you will be detained until the War is over. If, however, the war is over in less than one year, you may either be discharged at once or remain until you have completed a year's service, at your option }   17. *Yes*

I, *Alexander L Stanton* do solemnly declare that the above answers made by me to the above questions are true, and that I am willing to fulfil the engagements made.

Alexander L Stanton SIGNATURE OF RECRUIT.

W Hownsssm Signature of Witness.

OATH TO BE TAKEN BY RECRUIT ON ATTESTATION.

I, *Alexander L. Stanton* do make Oath, that I will be faithful and bear true Allegiance to Her Majesty, Her Heirs, and Successors, and that I will, as in duty bound, honestly and faithfully defend Her Majesty, Her Heirs, and Successors, in Person, Crown, and Dignity against all enemies, and will observe and obey all orders of Her Majesty, Her Heirs, and Successors, and of the Generals and Officers set over me. So help me God.

CERTIFICATE OF MAGISTRATE OR ATTESTING OFFICER.

The Recruit above-named was cautioned by me that if he made any false answer to any of the above questions he would be liable to be punished as provided in the Army Act.

The above questions were then read to the recruit in my presence.

I have taken care that he understands each question, and that his answer to each question has been duly entered as replied to, and the said recruit has made and signed the declaration and taken the oath before me at *Watford* on this *18th* day of *June* 1900 *G. Smith-Bosanquet Capt.* Signature of the Justice

Herts

If any alteration is required on this page of the Attestation, a Justice of the Peace should be requested to make it and initial the alteration under Section 80 (6), Army Act.

The Recruit should, if he require it, receive a copy of the Declaration on Army Form B. 112.

Fig 14a-14d Imperial Yeomanry Attestation Papers - Private Alexander Lee Stanton. (WO 128/20)

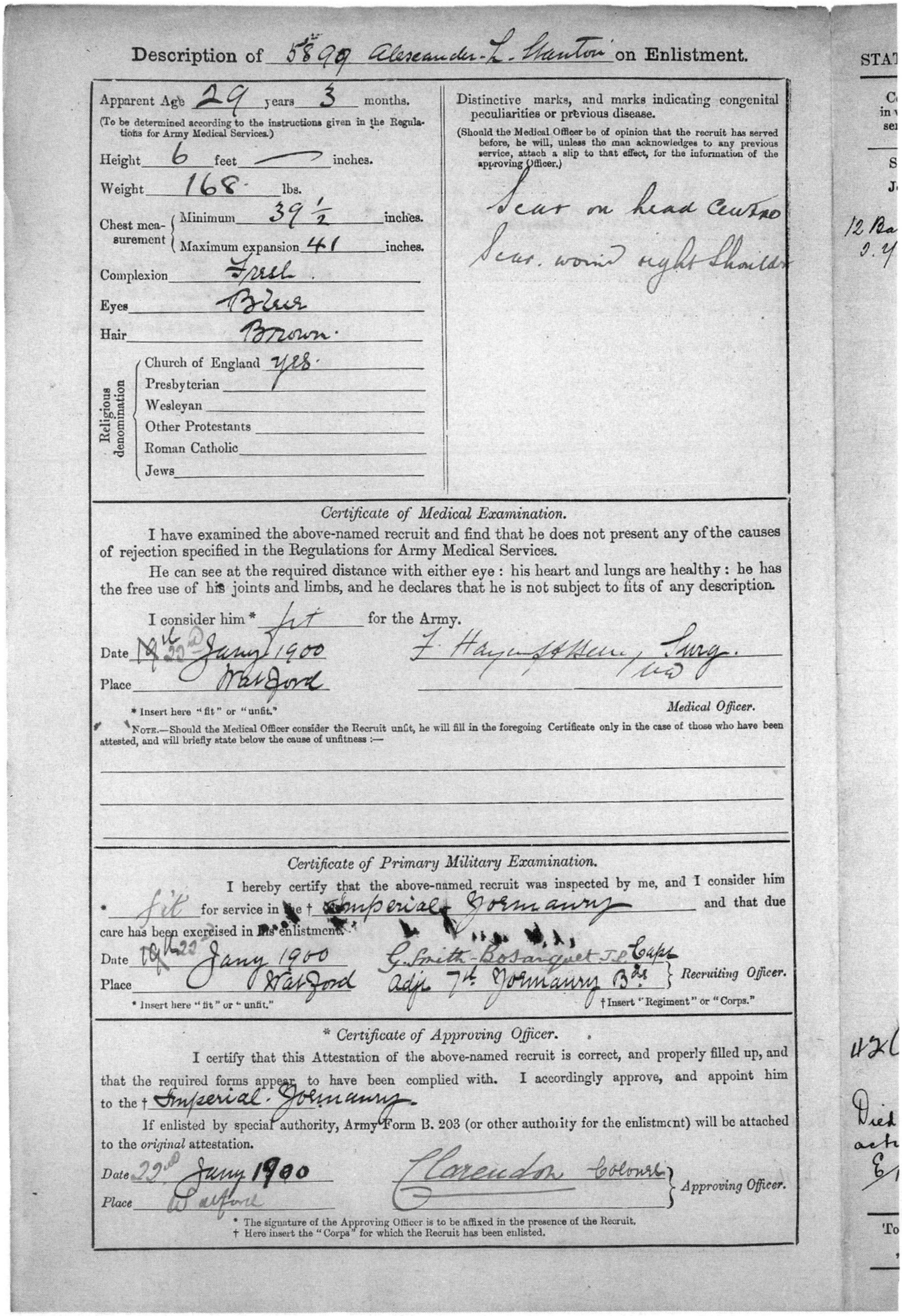

Description of 5899 *Alexander L. Stanton* on Enlistment.   STAT

Apparent Age 29 years 3 months.	**Distinctive marks, and marks indicating congenital peculiarities or previous disease.**
(To be determined according to the instructions given in the Regulations for Army Medical Services.)	(Should the Medical Officer be of opinion that the recruit has served before, he will, unless the man acknowledges to any previous service, attach a slip to that effect, for the information of the approving officer.)

Height 6 feet — inches.

Weight 168 lbs.

Chest measurement { Minimum 39½ inches. / Maximum expansion 41 inches. }

Complexion Fresh.

Eyes Blue

Hair Brown.

Scar on head Centro

Scar. wound right Shoulder

12 Ba
2.4

Religious denomination
- Church of England Yes.
- Presbyterian
- Wesleyan
- Other Protestants
- Roman Catholic
- Jews

Certificate of Medical Examination.

I have examined the above-named recruit and find that he does not present any of the causes of rejection specified in the Regulations for Army Medical Services.

He can see at the required distance with either eye : his heart and lungs are healthy : he has the free use of his joints and limbs, and he declares that he is not subject to fits of any description.

I consider him * fit for the Army.

Date 22 Jany 1900 F. Hayes Hen, Surg.

Place Watford

Medical Officer.

* Insert here "fit" or "unfit."

Note.—Should the Medical Officer consider the Recruit unfit, he will fill in the foregoing Certificate only in the case of those who have been attested, and will briefly state below the cause of unfitness :—

Certificate of Primary Military Examination.

I hereby certify that the above-named recruit was inspected by me, and I consider him * fit for service in the † Imperial Yeomanry and that due care has been exercised in his enlistment.

Date 22 Jany 1900 G. Smith-Bosanquet J.P Capt

Place Watford Adjt 7th Yeomanry B{ Recruiting Officer.

* Insert here "fit" or "unfit." † Insert "Regiment" or "Corps."

* Certificate of Approving Officer.

I certify that this Attestation of the above-named recruit is correct, and properly filled up, and that the required forms appear to have been complied with. I accordingly approve, and appoint him to the † Imperial Yeomanry.

If enlisted by special authority, Army Form B. 203 (or other authority for the enlistment) will be attached to the *original* attestation.

Date 22d Jany 1900 Clarendon Colonel{ Approving Officer.

Place Watford

* The signature of the Approving Officer is to be affixed in the presence of the Recruit.
† Here insert the "Corps" for which the Recruit has been enlisted.

426

Diet
act

To

Fig 14b

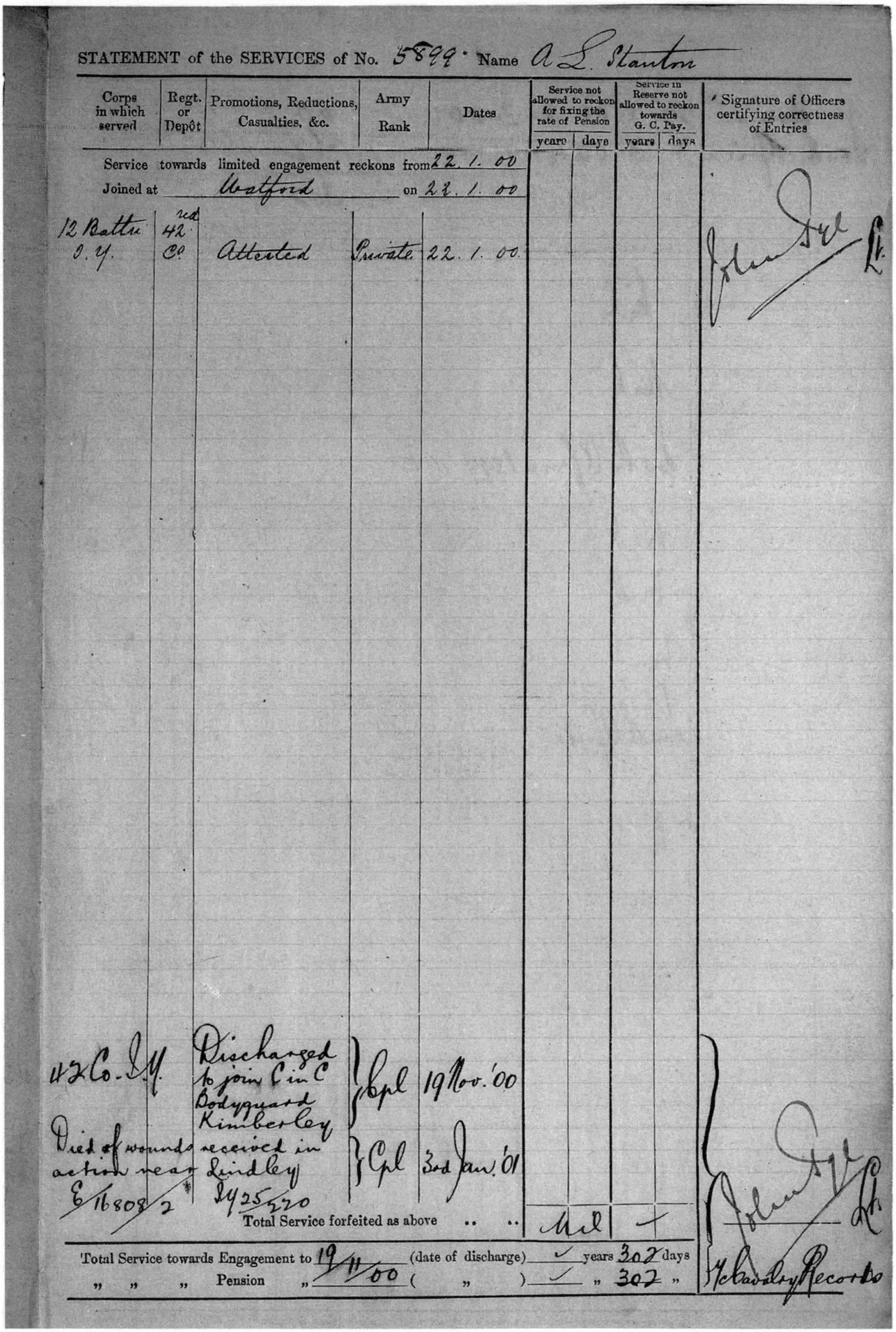

STATEMENT of the SERVICES of No. *5899* Name *A. L. Stanton*

Corps in which served	Regt. or Depôt	Promotions, Reductions, Casualties, &c.	Army Rank	Dates	Service not allowed to reckon for fixing the rate of Pension		Service in Reserve not allowed to reckon towards G. C. Pay.		Signature of Officers certifying correctness of Entries
					years	days	years	days	
		Service towards limited engagement reckons from *22. 1. 00*							
		Joined at *Watford* on *22. 1. 00*							*John Orr Lt.*
12 Batln. I.Y.	42nd Co.	Attested	Private	22. 1. 00					
42 Co. I.Y.		Discharged to join C in C Bodyguard Kimberley	Cpl	19 Nov. '00					
		Died of wounds received in action near Lindley	Cpl	3rd Jan. '01					*John Orr Lt.*
E/6808/2		2425570 Total Service forfeited as above					Nil		*Infantry Records*

Total Service towards Engagement to *19/11/00* (date of discharge) ✓ years *302* days
" " " Pension " *19/11/00* (") ✓ " *302* "

Fig 14c

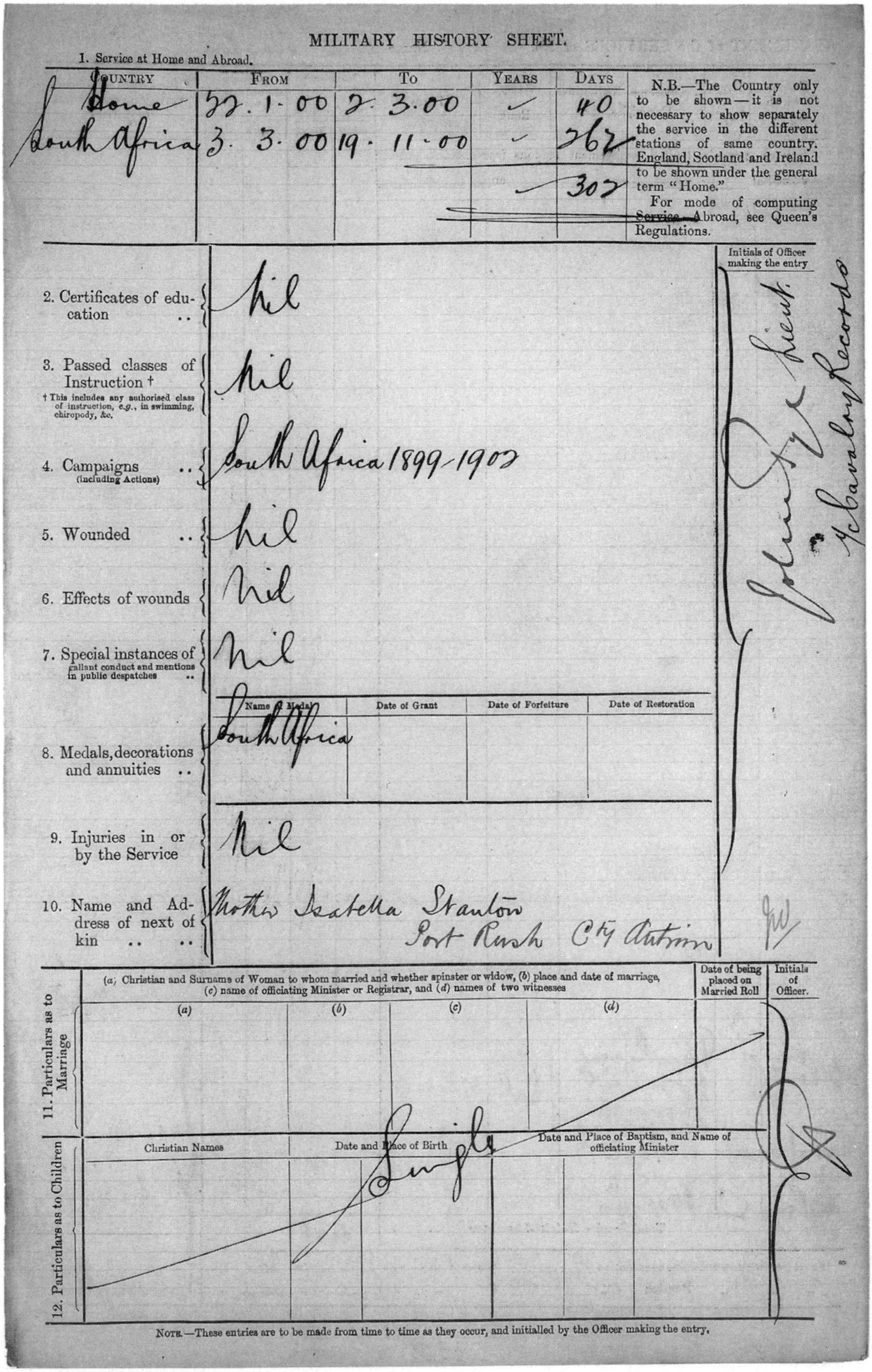

MILITARY HISTORY SHEET.

1. Service at Home and Abroad.

Country	From	To	Years	Days
Home	22. 1. 00	2. 3. 00	–	40
South Africa	3. 3. 00	19. 11. 00	–	262
			–	302

N.B.—The Country only to be shown—it is not necessary to show separately the service in the different stations of same country. England, Scotland and Ireland to be shown under the general term "Home."
For mode of computing Service Abroad, see Queen's Regulations.

Initials of Officer making the entry: John Eyre Lieut. 4 Cavalry Records

2. Certificates of education .. Nil

3. Passed classes of Instruction † Nil

† This includes any authorised class of instruction, *e.g.*, in swimming, chiropody, &c.

4. Campaigns (including Actions) .. South Africa 1899-1902

5. Wounded .. Nil

6. Effects of wounds Nil

7. Special instances of gallant conduct and mentions in public despatches .. Nil

8. Medals, decorations and annuities ..

Name of Medal	Date of Grant	Date of Forfeiture	Date of Restoration
South Africa			

9. Injuries in or by the Service Nil

10. Name and Address of next of kin .. .. Mother Isabella Stanton Port Rush Cty Antrim — JW

11. Particulars as to Marriage

(a) Christian and Surnames of Woman to whom married and whether spinster or widow, (b) place and date of marriage, (c) name of officiating Minister or Registrar, and (d) names of two witnesses — Date of being placed on Married Roll — Initials of Officer.

(a)	(b)	(c)	(d)	Date of being placed on Married Roll	Initials of Officer
Single					

12. Particulars as to Children

Christian Names	Date and Place of Birth	Date and Place of Baptism, and Name of officiating Minister

Note.—These entries are to be made from time to time as they occur, and initialled by the Officer making the entry.

Fig 14d

5
ROYAL ARTILLERY

5.1 Introduction

The Royal Artillery was formed in 1716. The Royal Horse Artillery, which was originally part of it, was established in 1793. Until 1855 the Royal Artillery was under the control of the Ordnance Office rather than the War Office. As a result, many of its records were kept separately and this separation is reflected in the current arrangement of the records, where much material relating to the Royal Artillery can be found in classes containing records relating to the Ordnance Office. They wore blue uniforms rather than red, had a separate pay system and, until 1834, drew their pensions from the Board of Ordnance rather than Chelsea.

Marriage and birth registers for the Royal Artillery between 1817 and 1827, 1860 and 1877 are in WO 69/551-582.

5.2 Officers

A published *List of Officers of the Royal Regiment of Artillery*, 1716-June 1914 (3 vols, London 1899, 1914) is available at Kew.

Records of service of officers, 1770-1870, are included in WO 76, for which there is an incomplete name index in the Research Enquiries Room - see section 3.6.2. Earlier lists of officers, 1727-1751, are in WO 54/684, 701. Pay lists for officers, 1803-1871, are in WO 54/946.

Other records include an incomplete series of commission books, 1740-1852, in WO 54/237-239, 244-247 and of officers for 1793 in WO 54/701. Original patents and warrants of appointment, 1670-1855, are in WO 54/939-945. Appointment papers for officers, 1809-1852, are in WO 54/917-922.

There are registers for officers receiving half pay between 1810 and 1880 in WO 23/82. For further details of half pay see section 3.7.

June's Woolwich Journal was a newspaper for the Royal Artillery at Woolwich. It contained news of officers, their movements with other interesting information. The PRO holds copies only for 1847 to 1850 in WO 62/48.

5.3 Other Ranks

Records of service of soldiers in the Royal Artillery, 1791-1855, are in WO 69. They include attestation papers and show name, age, description, place of birth, trade, and dates of service, of promotions, of marriage and of discharge or death. These records are arranged under the unit in which the individual last served, which can be ascertained from indexes and posting books in WO 69/779-782, 801-839.

Soldiers' documents for men of the Royal Artillery discharged to pension between 1760 and 1854 are in WO 97, although there appear to be very few documents earlier than 1792.

Muster rolls for the Royal Artillery, 1708-1878, are in WO 10; an example is illustrated as **figure 15**. Except for a few rolls, mostly for the eighteenth century, battalions which served in India are not included. Some later muster rolls are in WO 16.

Entry books of discharges, transfers and casualties between 1740 and 1858 are in WO 54/317-328. Casualty returns from 1850 are in WO 25.

There is also an incomplete series of registers of deceased, discharged or deserted men, 1772-1774, 1816-1873, in WO 69/583-597, 644-647, arranged by artillery regiment. Description books for Royal Artillery battalions between 1749 and 1859 are in WO 54/260-309, and for depots between 1773 and 1874 in WO 69/74-80. Books for the Royal Irish Artillery, 1756-1774, are in WO 69/620. A number of miscellaneous pay lists and other records of the Royal Artillery, 1692-1876, are in WO 54/672-755.

Registers of pensions, 1816-1833, are in WO 54/338-452, 470-480. Registers of pensions being paid in 1834, when responsibility for them was transferred from the Board of Ordnance to the Royal Hospital Chelsea, are in WO 23/141-145. In addition, there is in WO 116/127-185 a special series of admission books for Royal Artillery pensions between 1833 and 1913.

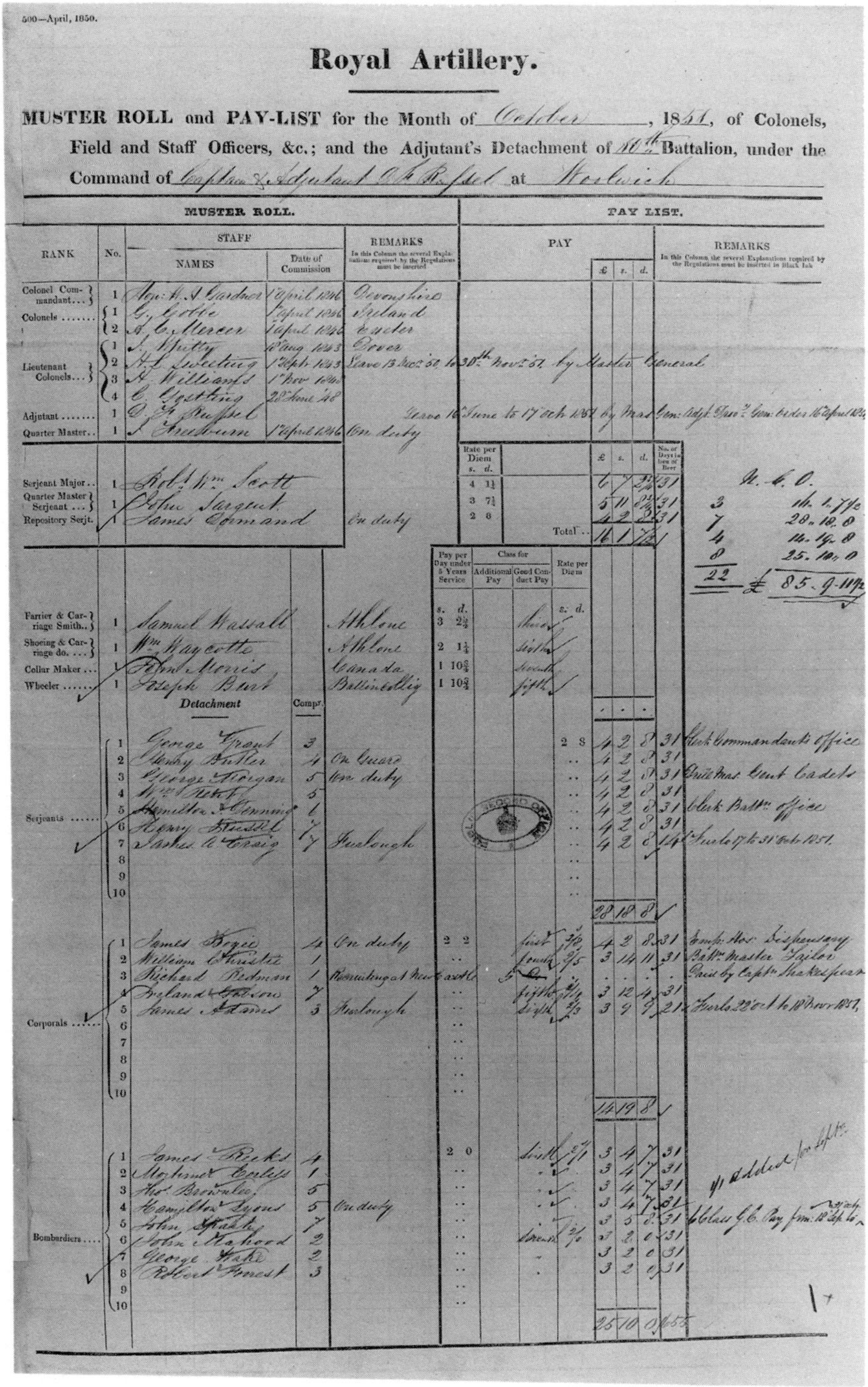
500—April, 1850.

Royal Artillery.

MUSTER ROLL and **PAY-LIST** for the Month of October, 1851, of Colonels, Field and Staff Officers, &c.; and the Adjutant's Detachment of 10th Battalion, under the Command of Captain & Adjutant O. Ft. Russel at Woolwich

MUSTER ROLL. | PAY LIST.

RANK	No.	STAFF NAMES	Date of Commission	REMARKS (In this Column the several Explanations required by the Regulations must be inserted)	PAY £	s.	d.	REMARKS (In this Column the several Explanations required by the Regulations must be inserted in Black Ink)
Colonel Commandant	1	Sir H. A. Gardner	1 April 1846	Devonshire				
Colonels	1	G. Cobbe	1 April 1846	Ireland				
	2	A. C. Mercer	1 April 1846	Exeter				
Lieutenant Colonels	1	J. Whitty	9 Aug 1843	Dover				
	2	H. L. Sweeting	1 Apr 1843	Leave 13 Dec 50 to 30th Nov 51 by Master General				
	3	H. Williams	1 Nov 1846					
	4	C. Gostling	28 June 48					
Adjutant	1	O. Ft. Russel		Leave 16 June to 17 Oct 1851 by Mas Gen: Adjt. Gen. Order 16 April 1851				
Quarter Master	1	J. Freeburn	1 April 1846	On duty				

RANK	No.	NAMES	Remarks	Rate per Diem s. d.	£	s.	d.	No. of Days
Serjeant Major	1	Robt. Wm. Scott		4 1½	6	7	2½	31
Quarter Master Serjeant	1	John Sargent		3 7¼	5	11	8¾	31
Repository Serjt.	1	James Cormand	On duty	2 8	4	2	8	31
				Total	16	1	7½	

RANK	No.	NAMES	Remarks	Pay per Day under 5 Years Service s. d.	Class for Good Conduct Pay
Farrier & Carriage Smith	1	Samuel Wassall	Athlone	3 2½	third
Shoeing & Carriage do.	1	Wm. Waycotte	Athlone	2 1¼	sixth
Collar Maker	1	John Morris	Canada	1 10¾	seventh
Wheeler	1	Joseph Burt	Ballincollig	1 10¾	fifth

RANK	No.	Detachment	Compy.	Remarks	Rate per Diem	£	s.	d.	Days	Remarks
Serjeants	1	George Grant	3		2 8	4	2	8	31	Clerk Commandant's Office
	2	Henry Butler	4	On Guard	..	4	2	8	31	
	3	George Morgan	5	On duty	..	4	2	8	31	Drill Mas. Gent Cadets
	4	Wm. Abbot	5		..	4	2	8	31	
	5	Hamilton Cumming	1		..	4	2	8	31	Clerk Battn. Office
	6	Henry Russell	7		..	4	2	8	31	
	7	James A. Craig	7	Furlough	..	4	2	8	14	Furlo 17 to 31 Octr 1851
	8				..					
	9				..					
	10					28	18	8		
Corporals	1	James Boyce	4	On duty	2 2	4	2	8	31	Hosp. Dispensary
	2	William Christie	1		..	3	14	11	31	Battn. Master Tailor
	3	Richard Redman	1	Recruiting at Newcastle	..	.	.	.		Paid by Captn. Shakespear
	4	Ireland Gibson	7		..	3	12	4	31	
	5	James Adams	3	Furlough	..	3	9	9	21	Furlo 22 Oct to 10 Nov 1851
	6–10				..					
						14	19	8		
Bombardiers	1	James Ricks	4		2 0	3	4	7	31	
	2	Mortimer Corliss	1		..	3	4	7	31	
	3	Thos. Brownlee	5		..	3	4	7	31	
	4	Hamilton Lyons	5	On duty	..	3	4	7	31	
	5	John Strahan	7		..	3	5	8	31	6 Class G.C. Pay
	6	John Mahood	2		..	3	2	0	31	
	7	George Wake	2		..	3	2	0	31	
	8	Robert Forrest	3		..	3	2	0	31	
	9–10				..					
						25	10	0		

16. 1. 7½
28. 18. 0
14. 19. 8
25. 10. 0
£ 85. 9. 11½

Fig 15 Muster Roll of the Adjutant's Detachment of the 10th Battalion, Royal Artillery, October 1851. (WO 10/2086)

5.4 Royal Horse Artillery

Records of service of soldiers in the Royal Horse Artillery, 1803-1863, are in WO 69. Description books for the Royal Horse Artillery between 1776 and 1821 are in WO 69/1-6.

A number of application papers for posts in the Royal Horse Artillery between 1820 and 1851 are in WO 54/927. Baptism and marriage registers between 1859 and 1883 are in WO 69/63-73.

6

ROYAL ENGINEERS

6.1 Introduction

The Corps of Engineers, consisting of officers only, was established as part of the Board of Ordnance in 1717. In 1772 a Corps of Royal Military Artificers was formed, to which other ranks were recruited. In 1811 it became the Royal Corps of Sappers and Miners. The two Corps merged to form the Royal Engineers in 1856. Many documents relating to Sappers and Miners are described in the lists as relating to Royal Engineers.

6.2 Officers

Engineer officers were until 1855 the responsibility not of the War Office but of the Board of Ordnance. Lists of engineer officers for 1793 are in WO 54/701. Registers of the establishment of the Royal Engineers for 1851 and 1855 are in WO 54/235-236. Commission books for officers, 1755-1852, are in WO 54/240-247. Returns of officers, showing stations where they were based between 1786 and 1850, are in WO 54/248-259. Appointment papers of officers, 1815-1846, are in WO 54/923-924. Pay lists for officers, 1805-1871, are in WO 54/947.

Records of service, 1796-1922, are in WO 25/3913-3919. These records include marriages and details of children of officers. An incomplete card index to these records is available in the Research Enquiries Room at Kew. Reports on students at the School of Military Engineering at Chatham, 1858-1914, are in WO 25/3945-3954. The register of cadets of the Royal Military Academy at Woolwich is in the class WO 149 but is held by the Royal Military Academy at Sandhurst and not at the PRO.

There are registers of officers receiving half pay between 1810 and 1880 in WO 23/82. For further details of half pay see section 3.7.

A list of officers has been published for the Royal Engineers called the *Roll of Officers of the Corps of Royal Engineers from 1660 to 1898* (London, 1898). A copy is available at Kew.

Service records of officers who served in the Supply and Service Department of the Royal Engineers between 1828 and 1903 are in WO 25/3921-3922.

6.3 Other Ranks

Soldiers' documents for 1760 to 1854 are in WO 97/1148-1152, and from 1855 to 1872 in WO 97/1359-1364. For further information about soldiers' documents see section 4.3.

A register of deceased soldiers in both the Royal Engineers and the Royal Corps of Sappers and Miners, 1824-1858, is in WO 25/2972, and an abstract of effects and credits of deceased men for 1825 in WO 25/2973. Entry books of discharges, transfers and casualties for artificers, sappers and miners and Royal Engineers between 1800 and 1859 are in WO 54/329-335.

A return of sappers and miners entitled to pensions in 1830 is in WO 54/482. Registers of sapper and miner pensioners, compiled in 1834 but dating back to the Napoleonic Wars, are in WO 23/141-145; they include descriptions of individuals. Description books for sappers, miners and artificers, 1756-1833, are in WO 54/310-316.

Musters and pay lists for the Royal Corps of Sappers and Miners and the Engineers between 1816 and 1878 are in WO 11. Further details about muster rolls are in section 4.4.

7

MILITIA, YEOMANRY AND VOLUNTEERS

7.1 Introduction

The militia was a trained local part-time force, with its origins in the middle ages, for home defence in time of rebellion or invasion. Section 2.2 describes the Tudor and Stuart militia and the records it created.

The Militia Act 1757 re-established one or more regiments for each county, raised from volunteers and conscripts chosen by ballot from each parish. Until 1871, the raising and training of local militias was the responsibility of the Lord Lieutenant of the county, who also appointed officers. In peacetime the militia assembled for drill and manoeuvres at intervals and after 1782 they came under the ultimate authority of the Home Secretary. In wartime, however, having been mobilized (or embodied) by royal proclamation, they were subject to the orders of the commander in chief and were liable to serve anywhere in the British Isles but not overseas, although in wartime individuals and whole units, might be encouraged to do so.

Other auxiliary forces formed in the late eighteenth and early nineteenth centuries were the Yeomanry, a cavalry corps; the Volunteers, raised by private or municipal enterprise for local defence; and the Local Militia. The Volunteers were dissolved in 1813 and the Local Militia in 1816 but the Yeomanry continued, mainly acting as an armed police force until its establishment was drastically reduced in 1859.

The Fencible Infantry and Cavalry, which were regular regiments raised for home service only, are often classed with the militia.

In 1859, as a result of local pressure and fears of a possible foreign invasion, volunteer regiments were again formed. They had little formal connection with the War Office until 1873. Thereafter, a small number of soldiers (including officers) or retired soldiers formed a permanent staff on each of these regiments.

After the reorganization of the Army on a territorial basis in 1881, the county militia regiments became the third battalions and the volunteer units the fourth and sometimes the fifth battalions of their local regiments. In 1908 the Militia was renamed the Special Reserve and the Volunteers and the Yeomanry became the Territorial Force. Men in the Territorial Force were only liable to serve within the United Kingdom but individuals might volunteer to serve abroad. Those in the Special Reserve had the same liability as ordinary Army Reservists of being called out for permanent service at home or abroad in an emergency. Both had to undergo annual training. In 1924 the Special Reserve was renamed the Supplementary Reserve which was not finally disbanded until 1953. In 1940 the Local Defence Volunteers, renamed the Home Guard, was formed for Home Defence. Stood down in December 1945, it was re-formed in 1952 and finally wound up in 1957.

7.2 Officers

Information about appointment of officers to militia and volunteer units from 1782 to 1840 can be found in the Home Office Military Papers (HO 50), with related entry books in HO 51. The papers include some establishment and succession books, but there is no name index and in general no information is given beyond the names of officers and the dates of their commissions. From 1865 names of officers appear in the Army List.

Records of service of officers in a number of militia regiments are in WO 68. They date from about 1757 to 1925, but are incomplete. Provided that the unit is known, it is possible to get a rough idea of an officer's service from the muster books in WO 13. Registers of pensions paid to militia officers, 1868-1892, are in WO 23/89-92. A selection of birth and baptismal certificates from 1788 to 1886 is in WO 32/8906-8913.

7.3 Other Ranks

The most useful records for the family historian are the attestation forms of those men who served in the militia, which are in WO 96. They range in date from 1806 to 1915, but the majority are from the second half of the nineteenth century. They are arranged alphabetically by surname order under the name of the regular regiment to which the militia unit was attached. In form and content they are similar to soldiers' documents, which are described in section 4.3. A number of soldiers' documents for men who served in militia regiments between 1760 and 1854 are in WO 97/1091-1112. They are arranged in name order, and appear to be mainly for Irish regiments. Very few of them date from before 1792.

Muster books and pay lists of the English, Scottish, Irish and Colonial Militia, and the Fencible Infantry and Cavalry, Yeomanry, Irish Yeomanry and Volunteers from 1780 to 1878 are in WO 13. Muster books and pay lists provide a means of establishing the dates of enlistment and discharge or death. When an individual appears for the first time the entry in the muster book may show his age. For volunteer units only, payments to the professional cadre, and not the ordinary volunteers, are included. Muster books are of use only if you know which unit your ancestor belonged to.

A list of Chelsea pensioners discharged from militia and yeomanry regiments between 1821 and 1829 is in WO 23/25.

Accounts and vouchers of payments to militiamen, their families and dependents may survive in E 182 with the records of the Receivers of the Land Tax, out of which such payments were made, eg from 1798 the families of militiamen serving in Ireland were provided with a bounty of 8 pence per week per wife and child under ten. These records are arranged topographically and are not listed in detail.

Records relating to men who served in the Imperial Yeomanry during the South African (Boer) War are described in section 12.4 and in the case study of Private A L Stanton in section 4.9.4.

7.4 Further Information

Few records of individual units of Militia, Yeomanry, Volunteers, Territorials or Home Guard are to be found in the Public Record Office. They are more likely to be found in local record offices, often with the private papers of Lords Lieutenant and other local notables who served as officers. An example of the type of records more commonly found locally is the Bosanquet Papers (PRO 30/3) which include the minute books, orderly books and reports of the Light Horse Volunteers of London and Westminster 1779-1831.

The main source of militia records is in WO 68. They include order books, succession books, records of officers' services, regimental histories and enrolment books.

A number of muster books for units based in London and Middlesex are in WO 70. Records for a few provincial units are in WO 79. Records of the Tower Hamlets Militia are in WO 94. There are some general Militia accounts in WO 9 and records relating to allowances for Militia, Yeomanry and Volunteers, 1793-1831 are in PMG 73.

Many records of militia and volunteer units are preserved at local record offices. These records are described in Jeremy Gibson and Mervyn Medlycott, *Militia lists and musters, 1757-1876* (FFHS, 1994). For further details of other record offices, see appendix 4 below.

For more detailed study of records relating to Militia and Volunteers Forces, together with the Home Guard, see *Records of the Militia and Volunteer Forces 1757-1945*, revised edition by W Spencer (PRO Readers' Guide No 3, 1997).

8

CAMPAIGNS AND CASUALTY RETURNS

8.1 Introduction

Records of units and formations engaged in particular campaigns are listed in detail in Michael Roper's *The Records of the War Office and related departments 1660-1964* (PRO, 1998). The record class SP 87 State Papers Foreign, Military Expeditions, contains correspondence of the Secretary of State, mainly with military commanders in the field, for the period 1695 to 1763. Individuals who served in particular campaigns may be traced through the awards of campaign medals - see section 9.3.

8.2 Casualties

There are several series of monthly and quarterly casualty returns for both officers and ordinary soldiers, arranged by regiment, in WO 25. These returns are dated between 1809 and 1910 and many are indexed. They give name; rank; place of birth; trade; the date, place and nature of the casualty; debts and credits; and next of kin or legatee. The returns in WO 25/3250-3260 cover the period 1842-1872 and include details of men discharged or who had deserted.

A series of entry books of casualties, 1797-1817, from the Muster Master General's Office is in WO 25/1196-1358. These books give the names in alphabetical order with details of cause of death and any financial credits the deceased might have had.

Nominal rolls of casualties were kept for many of the campaigns in which the Army fought during the second half of the nineteenth century. These rolls include the names of officers as well as other ranks.

Campaign	Date	Reference
Burma	1888	WO 25/3473
China	1857-1858	WO 32/8221, 8224, 8227
	1860	WO 32/8230, 8233-8234
China (Tsingtao)	1915	WO 32/4996B
Egypt	1882, 1884	WO 25/3473
New Zealand	1860	WO 32/8255
	1863-1864	WO 32/8263-8268, 8271, 8276-8280
Sierra Leone	1898	WO 32/7630-7631
South Africa	1878-1881	WO 25/3474, WO 32/7700, 7706-7708, 7727, 7819
	1899-1902	WO 108/89-91, 338
Sudan	1884-1885	WO 25/3473, WO 32/6123, 6125-6126, 8382

Several casualty lists have been published eg: Frank and Andrea Cook, *The Casualty Roll for the Crimea* (London, 1976); John Young, *'They Fell like Stones': casualties of the Zulu War, 1879* (1991); *South Africa Field Force Casualty List, 1899-1902* (London, 1972), a facsimile of WO 108/338; Mildred C Donner, *The Last Post being a roll of all Officers (Naval, Military and Colonial) who gave their names for Queen, King and Country in the South Africa War, 1899-1902* (1903, reprinted 1980) and R W Walker, *To what end did they die? Officers who died at Gallipoli* (1985).

Other records relating to casualties include registers of authorities to deal with effects, 1810-1822, in WO 25/2966-2971 (recording name, regiment, date of death, amount of effects and credits and the name and address of the person, usually next of kin, applying for them); an index to effects, 1830, in WO 25/2974; a register of effects and credits, 1830-1844, in WO 25/2975; and record book of effects 1862-1881 in WO 25/3476-3490, indexed by WO 25/3491-3501. Papers relating to Artillery and Engineer deaths and effects, 1824-1859, are in WO 25/2972-2973, 2976-2978. WO 334 includes annual death and disability returns for 1817-1892 which give the names of individuals.

9

MEDALS AND AWARDS, 1793-1967

9.1 Introduction

Medals and awards can be split into four basic groups: awards for gallantry or meritorious service, campaign medals, long service medals and awards to commemorate specific events.

9.2 Awards for Gallantry or Meritorious Service

Although various distinctions have been bestowed upon individuals for their deeds performed during peace or wartime, it is only since the Victorian era that awards for gallantry or meritorious service have been bestowed on a more liberal and regular basis.

Apart from the highest orders of chivalry, the most frequently bestowed order of chivalry in the early nineteenth century was the Most Honourable Order of the Bath (1725). The records of appointments to the Order of the Bath can be found in WO 103.

The war against Russia in the Crimea bought about the creation of two gallantry awards. The Distinguished Conduct Medal (DCM) was instituted in 1854. Submissions for awards of the DCM made between 1854 and 1901 are in WO 146. Further files about the DCM can be found in WO 32 code 50S. The register of the DCM providing a name index of awards granted between 1855 and 1920 is in WO 391, available on microfilm in the Microfilm Reading Room. Awards of the DCM granted between 1854 and 1909 are listed in P E Abbott, *Recipients of the Distinguished Conduct Medal 1855-1909* (London, 1992).

The Victoria Cross (VC) was instituted in February 1856 and was first awarded for acts of bravery performed during the Crimean War. The first VC was awarded to

Charles Lucas. Details relating to Victoria Crosses awarded between 1854 and 1914 can be found in WO 32 codes 50D and 50M. The Public Record Office has many books about the Victoria Cross please ask in the library.

The register of awards of the VC covering the period 1856-1957, together with the royal warrant instituting the award and submission for awards up to 1903, is in WO 98. Entries from the register relating to men who were awarded the Victoria Cross for gallantry at Rorke's Drift in 1879 are reproduced as **figure 16**. A list of recipients of the VC 1856-1946 is in CAB 106/320. Citations for the Victoria Crosses awarded during the Second World War are in CAB 106/312.

In 1886 the Distinguished Service Order (DSO) was instituted (WO 32/6278) as an award for distinguished service during campaigns and for acts of gallantry. Details about the DSO can be found in WO 32 code 52 D. Details of all awards of the DSO granted between 1886 and 1923 can be found in Sir O'Moore Creagh and Miss E Humphries, *Register of the DSO* (London, 1923), a copy of which is available in the Microfilm Reading Room.

Recommendations for awards made during the Boer War can be found in WO 108.

Most awards for distinguished service or gallantry made during the period 1855-1903 were announced in the *London Gazette*, available at major reference libraries and also at the PRO in the record class ZJ1. Not all awards announced in the *London Gazette* were accompanied by a citation and therefore you need to look at the primary sources in the PRO to discover why an individual was so honoured. Indexes covering this period, together with the relevant announcements, can be found in ZJ 1.

Awards created and awarded during the First World War are covered in *Army Service Records of the First World War*, S Fowler, W Spencer and S Tamblin (PRO Readers' Guide No 19 (1997)).

Recommendations for awards for gallantry or meritorious service for the period 1938-1967 can be found in the record class WO 373. This class, which is available on microfilm, is arranged by operational theatre in which the award was won and then in *London Gazette* date order. Awards for meritorious service which were announced in the 'Half Yearly' lists, the New Year or Birthday Honours can also be found in WO 373. Awards for service in Malaya, Korea and other post Second World War conflicts can also be found in WO 373. Awards for 'Combat Gallantry' include the VC, DSO, Military Cross (MC), DCM and Military Medal (MM). Awards for 'Non-Combat Gallantry' include the George Cross and George Medal. Awards for meritorious service include the CBE, OBE, MBE and BEM.

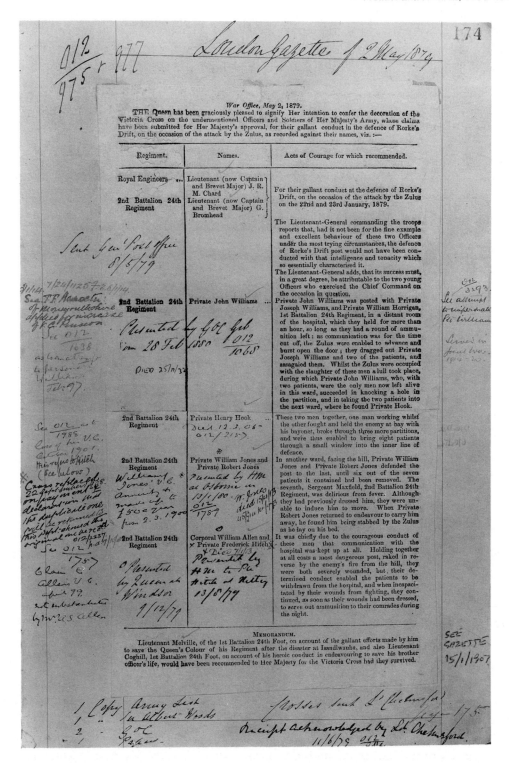

Fig 16 Register of Awards of the Victoria Cross, 1879. (WO 98/4, p 174)

Nurses who were awarded the Royal Red Cross (RRC) or Royal Red Cross 2nd Class (ARRC) during the Second World War can find the recommendations in WO 373. The register of the Royal Red Cross for the period 1883 to June 1918 can be found in WO 145/1.

9.3 Campaign Medals, 1793-1913

Although many commanding officers of various campaigns were given a medal to commemorate that particular campaign or battle, the modern era of campaign medals did not start until 1816, with the authorization of the Waterloo Medal for services the previous year. The Waterloo Medal is important in modern medallic history as it was the first medal given to all men irrespective of rank; it was the first medal to be stamped by machine and, as long as their next of kin applied for it, the first to be given to the families of men who died in the battle.

Although a number of other medals were awarded for campaigns around the globe, the next important medal to be instituted after the Waterloo Medal was the Military General Service Medal 1793-1814 (MGS). Authorized in 1847, the MGS was only issued to survivors of a number of battles which took place in the wars against France. As the medal was only issued to survivors alive in 1847, it is not common.

Details of all British campaign medals awarded for campaigns between 1793 and 1984 can be found in *British Battles and Medals*, E Joslin, A Litherland and B Simpkin (Spink 1988), copies of which are available in the Research Enquiries Room and the library.

9.3.1 Medal rolls

After a campaign or battle was over many campaign medals were authorized to be given to participating troops. In order to find out who was present at a particular campaign or battle, a roll of all those present or not, had to be taken. Once the roll was taken, a medal roll in the format laid down by the Army Order (WO 123) announcing the award was created. The medal rolls for all of these medal issues can be found in the record class WO 100 and are available on microfilm in the Microfilm Reading Room. An example is illustrated as **figure 17**. The WO 100 class list is arranged in chronological order of campaign or battle. Each medal roll is arranged in regimental order of precedence, ie the most senior regiment first, and then usually by rank and within these in alphabetical order.

A number of medal rolls have been published over the years, please ask in the library to see what is available. Apart from the War Office records, other sources relating to medals include the records of the Royal Mint, most notably the Waterloo Medal book which is in MINT 16/112.

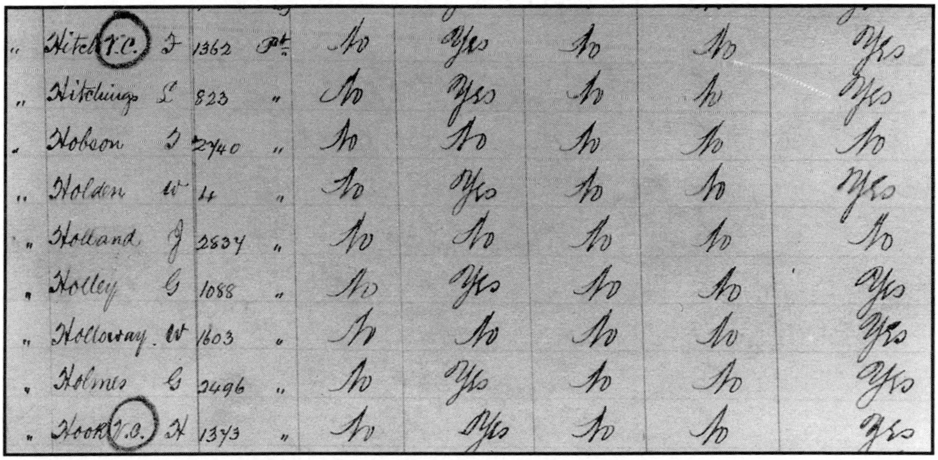

"	Hitch (V.C.)	F	1362	Pte	No	Yes	No	No	Yes
"	Hitchings	L	823	"	No	Yes	No	No	Yes
"	Hobson	J	2740	"	No	No	No	No	No
"	Holden	W	4	"	No	Yes	No	No	Yes
"	Holland	J	2537	"	No	No	No	No	No
"	Holley	G	1088	"	No	Yes	No	No	Yes
"	Holloway	W	1603	"	No	No	No	No	Yes
"	Holmes	G	2496	"	No	Yes	No	No	Yes
"	Hook (V.C.)	H	1373	"	No	Yes	No	No	Yes

Figure 17 Medal Roll, South Africa, 1879. (WO 100/46 pt 3, f 172v)

This example has columns, reading from left to right, for: rank; name; rank and regimental number at time medal awarded; whether in possession of the medal for previous wars; whether engaged against the Gaikas and other Kaffir tribes; whether engaged against Pokwane 1878; Whether engaged against the Griquas 1878; whether engaged against the Zulus 1879.

The campaign medal rolls for the First World War are in the record class WO 329, with a card index, available on microfiche in the record class WO 372. For a full explanation of these rolls, see *Army Service Records of the First World War*, (PRO Readers' Guide No 19, 1997) and section 16.5.

The PRO holds no medal rolls for campaigns after the First World War. All post 1918 medal rolls are still held by the Army Medal Office, Government Buildings, Worcester Road, Droitwich, Worçestershire, WR9 8AU.

9.3.2 Other sources on campaign medals

Apart from the records mentioned above, a number of other record classes contain lists of names relating to campaigns and their subsequent medal issue, these include;

Campaign	**Reference**	
Kurdistan (1925)	WO 32/3564	
New Zealand (1861, 1863)	WO 32/8258, 8270	
Nubia, Sudan (1926-1927)	WO 32/3537	
Rhodesia (1898)	WO 32/7840, 7842-7843	
Sierra Leone (1898)	WO 32/7629, 7632, 7635	cont....

Campaign	Reference
Somaliland (1903-1904)	WO 32/8428, 8440
South Africa (1878-1879)	WO 32/7682, 7764
South Africa (1899-1903)	WO 32/7960, WO 108/136-179
Sudan (1884-1886, 1896-1898)	WO 32/3539
Tsingtao, China (1914-1915)	WO 32/4996B

9.4 Long Service Medals

In 1833 a Long Service and Good Conduct Medal was instituted for soldiers who had served eighteen years in the Army. Medal rolls for this medal between 1831 and 1953 are in WO 102. Awards of long service medals to officers in colonial forces, 1891-1894, are in WO 32/8293-8298. WO 102 also contains some rolls for medals issued to men serving in militia and colonial forces.

In 1846 a Meritorious Service Medal was authorized for sergeants and warrant officers who had performed good service other than in battle. Awards for meritorious service between 1846 and 1919 are in WO 101. A register of annuities paid to recipients of the meritorious or long service awards, 1846-1879, is in WO 23/84. Rolls for the Volunteer Officers' Decoration, 1892-1932, are in WO 330.

9.5 Medal Commemorating Specific Events

A number of different medals have been awarded to members of the British Army over the last hundred years, such as medals commemorating the coronation or jubilee of a sovereign, or for marksmanship. Unfortunately rolls for most of these medal issues are not preserved amongst the records in the PRO. Those that are can be found in WO 100 and WO 32 code 50A.

9.6 Foreign Medals Awarded to British Soldiers

Since the Crimean War, and in a number of instances prior to that, foreign governments have sometimes awarded decorations to British servicemen. In most cases, the award to Britons of foreign decorations has been dealt with by the Treasury Department of the Foreign Office. Although a number of awards were announced in the *London Gazette*, in many cases it is the records in FO 83, FO 371 and FO 372 which need to be consulted. Those wishing to use these Foreign Office classes may need to seek further advice from staff in the Research Enquiries Room.

10

COURTS MARTIAL

10.1 Introduction

There were three different types of court martial for which the PRO holds records: general courts martial, general regimental courts martial (before 1829) and district courts martial (after 1829).

10.2 Officers

Tracing the courts martial of commissioned officers is relatively straightforward, since they could be tried only by general court martial. WO 93/1B is an index to trials of officers, 1806-1904. WO 93/1A is an index to general courts martial between 1806 and 1833.

There are three main types of record relating to individual trials: papers, proceedings and registers. Papers were compiled at the time of the court martial and are arranged in date order. They are in WO 71/121-343 and cover the period between 1688 and 1850, with one file for 1879. Other papers for trials between 1850 and 1914 were destroyed by enemy bombing in 1940. Papers for some special cases, mainly senior officers, are listed individually between 1780 and 1824 in WO 71/99-120, as are special returns for Ireland, 1800-1820, which are in WO 71/252-264. When papers reached the Judge Advocate General's Office, their contents were entered into the volumes of proceedings. They were kept in two series depending on whether the sentence was confirmed at home by the Sovereign, or abroad by a colonial governor or overseas commander. These records are in WO 71/13-98 and continued in WO 91. Until the mid-nineteenth century, the proceedings report the trials in detail, but later volumes give only the charges, findings and sentences in the form in which they were handed to the Sovereign. They also contain copies of warrants for the holding of courts martial and correspondence concerning the confirmation of sentences. Registers of warrants are in WO 28. The commander in chief's submissions upon sentence are in WO 209.

The Judge Advocate General's Office also compiled registers of courts martial, giving the name, rank, regiment, place of trial, charge, finding and sentence. Registers of courts martial confirmed abroad are in WO 90 and those confirmed at home are in WO 92. Records of field general courts martial date only from the South African War (1899-1902) and are combined in registers with district courts martial, for 1900 and 1901 only, in WO 92. Later registers, between 1909 and 1963, are in WO 213.

10.3 Other Ranks

NCOs and ordinary soldiers could be tried by general regimental courts martial (before 1829) and district courts martial (after 1829), as well as by general courts martial. As a result it is more difficult to find the records of individual cases. Only registers, rather than full proceedings, were compiled in the Judge Advocate General's Office. Registers of general regimental courts martial, between 1812 and 1829, are in WO 89 and of district courts martial, between 1829 and 1971, in WO 86. Both classes contain trials confirmed both at home and abroad, except those for London, 1865-1875, which are in WO 87, and India, 1878-1945, in WO 88. There are no records of minor offences tried by regimental courts martial, apart from the details which may be found on a soldier's regimental conduct sheet, found with his record of service.

For general courts martial the records are as described for officers above.

10.4 Other Sources

Records relating to individual cases are closed for seventy-five years from the date of the last entry in each piece. However, purely summary records of a more recent date are open. WO 93/40 gives particulars of death sentences carried out between 1941 and 1953. Nominal rolls of courts martial of all ranks of Australian and Canadian forces, 1915-1919, are in WO 93/42-45. A list of death sentences carried out in the British Army during the First World War is in WO 93/49. Nominal rolls of courts held in the Prisoners of War camp at Changi, 1942-1944, are in WO 93/46-48. Statistics for army and air force courts martial, 1914-1954, are in WO 93/49-59.

11

THE BRITISH ARMY IN INDIA AND THE INDIAN ARMY

11.1 Introduction

Until 1859 the army in India belonged to the East India Company and consisted of separate regiments of European and Indian troops led by European officers. The Company administered India through three Presidencies, Bengal, Madras and Bombay, each of which had its own army. In 1861, the European regiments became part of the British Army and the Indian troops became the Indian Army under the control of the viceroy in Delhi.

Service records for officers and soldiers of the East India Company army and its successors are, for the most part, held by the British Library, Oriental and India Office Collections. These include muster rolls and casualty returns for the Bengal army (1716-1861); the Madras army (1762-1861) and the Bombay army (1708-1865); records of pension funds, such as the Lord Clive Fund (from 1770) and registers of births, marriages and deaths. The Library also holds entry papers for officer cadets between 1789 and 1860. These papers include baptismal certificates and educational qualifications. Also kept by the Library are registers of recruits, 1817-1860, and embarkation lists, 1753-1861.

A brief description of the records held by the British Library is given in appendix 4. A Farrington's *Guide to the records of the India Office military department* (1982) is a detailed list of the military records held at the British Library, Oriental and India Office Collection which also holds published lists of East India Company army officers - *Indian Army Lists* and the *East India Register and Directory*, which was published annually from 1803.

11.2 East India Company and Indian Army

A few records relating to the East India Company and Indian Army are held by the PRO. Lists of officers of the European regiments, 1796-1841, are in WO 25/3215-3219.

Registers of service of every officer holding a commission on 1 November 1871 are in the papers of the Army Purchase Commission in WO 74, together with a series of applications from officers on Indian establishments, 1871-1891, to which certificates of service are attached. Papers and applications are indexed by regiment but not by name of applicant.

Registers and indexes of East India Company Army pensions, 1849-1876, and Indian Army pensions, 1849-1868, are in WO 23/17-23. A register of pensions paid to former soldiers serving with the East India Company between 1824 and 1856 is in WO 25/3137. Lists of deserters from the Company's army between 1844 and 1851 are in WO 25/2933.

War diaries of Indian Army formations during the First World War are in WO 95. War diaries for the Second World War are in WO 169 - WO 179.

11.3 British Army in India

Service records of officers and men serving with the British Army in India, as in other parts of the world, are described in chapters 3 and 4 above.

A list of British officers who served in India between 1796 and 1804 is in WO 25/3215. Records for soldiers discharged on return from India before 1806 will be found in the depot musters of their regiments (WO 67). Between 1863 and 1878 the discharges of men returning from India are recorded in the musters of the Victoria Hospital, Netley (WO 12/13077-13105); between 1862 and 1889 similar information is in the muster rolls of the Discharge Depot at Gosport (WO 16/2284, 2888-2915). Except for a few eighteenth-century artillery rolls, there are no musters of artillery and engineers in India, but musters of infantry and cavalry regiments in India between 1883 and 1889 are in WO 16/2751-2887.

11.4 Other Sources

Registers of the deaths of officers in all the Indian services for the Second World War are held by the British Library, Oriental and India Office Collections. Registers of garrison churches, and other churches used by soldiers and their families, are held by the diocesan authorities in India. Births, marriages and deaths for officers and men of the British Army in India appear in the Chaplain's Returns held at the Family Records Centre. Details of these records are given in appendix 4.

The National Army Museum holds Hodson's Index, a very large card index of British Officers in the Indian Army, the Bengal Army and the East India Company Army, but not the British Army in India. Many of the entries go beyond bare facts to include colourful stories of life. Civilians and government staff are included if they had seen army life. Details of the holdings of the National Army Museum are given in appendix 4.

Two useful books are V C P Hodgson, *Lists of Officers of the Bengal Army* (London, 1927-1928, revised 1968) and Byron Farwell, *Armies of the Raj* (London, 1990) which is a social history of the Indian Army.

12

COLONIAL AND DOMINIONS FORCES

12.1 Introduction, 1754-1902

Many colonial regiments were raised in the eighteenth and nineteenth centuries. Published histories of such units are noted in R Perkins, *Regiments and Corps of the British Empire and Commonwealth, a critical bibliography* (1994). References to individual officers and men may also occasionally be found in the appropriate records of the Colonial Office and its predecessors.

Soldiers' documents for men who served in colonial regiments between 1760 and 1872 are in WO 97. Microfilmed copies of these records for regiments raised, or primarily serving, in Canada are held by the National Archives of Canada, 395 Wellington Street, Ottawa, K1A 0N3 Canada. The National Archives of fomer colonies may hold other records relating to troops and militia forces stationed there - see section 12.5.

Muster books of certain colonial regiments are in WO 12 and those of colonial militia are in WO 13. Many men from the colonies, especially those of Canadian origin, served with the 100th Foot. Half pay returns for officers who had served in Canadian forces between 1783 and 1813 are in WO 24/748-762.

Returns of NCOs and men serving with colonial units in 1806 are in WO 25/1070-1121. Admission books for pensions payable in the colonies, 1817-1875, are in WO 23/147-152. There is an admission book for native and colonial pensioners, 1880-1903, in WO 23/160. Other registers of pensions paid to colonial soldiers are in WO 22. Casualty lists for colonial regiments between 1797 and 1817 are in WO 25/1345-1357, 2183-2207, 2242-2295, with indexes in WO 25/2689-2713, 2734-2753. Further indexes to casualty returns, 1850 to 1910, are in WO 25/3465-3471.

12.2 Records of Individual Colonial Regiments

There are description books for officers in the following regiments:

Unit	Date	Reference
Cape Mounted Rifles	1825-1865	WO 25/636-637
Ceylon Rifles	1809-1872	WO 25/638-641
Royal Canadian Rifles	1841-1868	WO 25/632-633
West India Rangers	1804-1816	WO 25/663
West India Regiments	1826-1869	WO 25/646-650 652, 660

In addition, returns of officers' services compiled in 1829 and 1872 for a number of regiments are in WO 25/805, 824, 840, 854 and 869. Further details about these records are in section 3.6.

Lists, registers and admission books for negro and Cape Mounted Rifle Corps pensioners, 1837-1879, are in WO 23/153-157, 159. Another admission book for men serving in the Ceylon Regiment and the Gun Lascars between 1868 and 1876 is in WO 23/158.

Lists of soldiers employed by the Royal African Company between 1756 and 1815 are in T 70/1454-1456. T 70 also contains a great deal of information about garrisons in West Africa.

For the period up to 1739 the printed *Calendars of State Papers Colonial*, which are indexed by personal name, may contain references to individual officers and men. Colonial Office records for the relevant country may contain some references to individual regiments and those who served in them such as the design of a proposed uniform for a soldier in the Cape of Good Hope Regiment, illustrated as **figure 18**, taken from CO 48 - Cape of Good Hope (Cape Colony) Original Correspondence.

12.3 North America

Lists of men who served in certain provincial volunteer forces in North America, 1746-1747, 1775-1783, are in WO 28/1, 4-5. Further muster rolls for militia units in the colonies of Connecticut, Massachusetts, New Hampshire and Rhode Island between 1759 and 1763 are in T 64/22. A list of officers who served in provincial forces during the American War of Independence is in T 64/23. Certificates of birth,

Fig 18 Uniform design for a soldier in the Cape of Good Hope Regiment, 1808. (CO 48/3)

baptism, marriage and death for a number of officers in Loyal American and Canadian units between 1776 and 1881 are in WO 42/59-63. Lists of men who served with the North and South Carolina militia are in T 50.

Some muster rolls of provincial loyalist troops in the American War of Independence are preserved in the National Archives of Canada, 395 Wellington Street, Ottawa, K1A 0N3 Canada.

12.4 South Africa, 1899-1902

Service records and attestation papers for men who served in locally recruited volunteer forces during the South African War (1899-1902) are in WO 126 and WO 127. Soldiers' documents for the Imperial Yeomanry are in WO 128. They are arranged by regimental number, which may be found in the indexes in WO 129/1-7. Casualties are recorded in WO 129/8-11 and WO 108/338. Details are also available in *South African Field Force Casualty List, 1899-1902* (London, 1972), which is available at Kew. For further information see *Militia and Volunteer Forces 1757-1945* by William Spencer (PRO, 1997). A case study of a man who served in the South African Local Forces is in section 4.9.4.

Records of men who served in Natal volunteer regiments or the militia between 1884 and 1912 are held by the Natal Archives Depot, Private Bag, X9012, 3200 Pietermaritzburg South Africa.

12.5 1902-1953

Records relating to members of colonial and dominion forces can sometimes be found among relevant records of the Colonial and Dominions Offices. Original correspondence relating to the King's African Rifles, which was formed in 1902 from the armed forces of various East African dependencies, is in CO 534, with registers in CO 623 and CO 624. Original correspondence for the Niger and West Africa Force, formed in 1897, is in CO 445, with registers in CO 581 and CO 582. From 1927 correspondence about various colonial forces is in CO 820.

War diaries of colonial and dominion forces for the First World War are in WO 95. Casualty records and medal rolls for Canadian forces in the South African and First World Wars are held by the Canadian Department of Veteran Affairs, Honours and Awards, 284 Wellington Street, Ottawa, K1A 0P4, Canada.

War diaries for colonial forces for the Second World War are in WO 169-WO 178. With the exception of Australia and Southern Rhodesia, war diaries for forces of the dominions are in WO 179. War diaries for Southern Rhodesian Forces are in WO 333. Australian war diaries are held by the Australian War Memorial, GPO Box 345, Canberra, ACT 2601 Australia.

CO 820/50/1-12 contain nominal rolls for British and European officers and other ranks serving with local forces in certain non-African colonies.

During the Korean War (1950-1953), the Commonwealth Division included several Australian and Canadian units. The war diaries for all these units are in WO 281.

Service records for men who served in the Australian armed forces after 1914 are held by the Historical Research Centre, Central Army Records Office, 360 St Kilda Road, Melbourne, VIC 3044 Australia. An extensive collection of material relating to all branches of the Australian fighting services is held by the Australian War Memorial, GPO Box 345, Canberra, ACT 2601 Australia. The War Memorial is unable to undertake genealogical research, but can supply the names of professional researchers to do the work for you. Their holdings are described in Joyce Bradley et al, *Roll call! A guide to genealogical sources in the Australian War Memorial* (Canberra, 1986).

Service records for Canadians who served during the two world wars are held by the Personnel Records Centre, National Archives of Canada, Tunney's Pasture, Ottawa, K1A 0N3 Canada.

Naval, army and air force service records for New Zealanders from 1899 are held by Base Records, Ministry of Defence, Private Bag, Wellington, New Zealand. Records held by the National Archives of New Zealand, PO Box 6148, Te Aro, Wellington include nineteenth-century material relating to British imperial troops, pensioner settlers, local militia and volunteer corps military settlers of the 1860s. More recent records include material on conscription, reservists and war diaries. These records are described in more detail in *Family History at the National Archives* (Wellington, NZ, 1990).

Service records for South African servicemen from 1912 are held by the Military Information Bureau, Archives Section, Private Bag X289, 0001 Pretoria, South Africa. The Bureau will do searches for family historians. The National Archives of South Africa, Private Bag X206, 0001 Pretoria hold some military records. Of particular interest are the personal files of the South African Constabulary which many British soldiers joined at the end of the South African War (1899-1902), usually for a short time before returning to England or going to another colony. These records are described in more detail in R T J Lombard, *Handbook for Genealogical Research in South Africa* (Pretoria, 1990).

The Commonwealth Forces History Trust, 37 Davis Road, London W3 7SE, may be able to help people interested in the history or records of colonial and dominion army units.

13

FOREIGN TROOPS IN
BRITISH PAY

13.1 Introduction

There have often been foreign troops in British pay and serving under British Command. Many of the records described elsewhere in this guide include information about foreign troops in British pay. In particular many foreigners, especially Germans, served with the 60th Foot.

13.2 1775-1816

Muster rolls of Hessian troops in British pay in North America, 1776-1794 and 1796-1797, are in AO 3/55, 58-59. Pay lists between 1775 and 1795 are in T 38/812-814. An index of names is available at Kew. Nominal rolls of Hessian troops may also be found in WO 12, WO 28/12, CO 5/139-140, 182-184 and HO 50/452. Further information about these Hessian soldiers may be obtained from the Institut fuer Archivwissenschaft, Archivschule Marburg, D-3550 Marburg an der Lahn, Germany.

Muster rolls of French royalist forces in British pay during the Napoleonic Wars are amongst the Bouillon papers in HO 69. Musters and pay lists for officers in the French Emigrant Engineers and Artillery are in WO 54/702.

Some birth, baptism, marriage and death certificates for officers in French, Greek, Swiss and Italian Corps are in WO 42/64-65. They cover the period between 1776 and 1881, but are mostly from the Napoleonic War period.

Statements were taken in June 1806 of the period of service of all NCOs and men in certain French refugee units. Those for the Chasseurs Britanniques are in WO 25/

1099 and for Dillon's and Meuron's Regiments in WO 25/1116-1117. A list of men discharged from foreign regiments between 1783 and 1810 is in WO 25/1121.

Casualty returns for foreign troops between 1809 and 1816 are in WO 25/2267-2271, 2289-2292, with indexes in WO 25/2753, 2892. Muster rolls of foreign regiments are in WO 12. Those for units of foreign artillery are in WO 10.

Histories of foreign regiments in the British army, 1793-1802, are given in the *Journal of the Society for Army Historical Research* vol 22 (1943-1944).

13.3 King's German Legion

Soon after the resumption of the Napoleonic Wars in 1803 attempts were made to recruit foreign troops to serve in the British Army. The Hanoverian army had been disbanded under the terms of the Treaty of Amiens, and special efforts were made by the British to recruit former members of this army. Virtually all members of the King's German Legion came from Hanover. The Legion fought in the Baltic, in Spain, and in Southern France. In 1815 it took part in the Battle of Waterloo. It was disbanded in 1816 and many of the officers and men joined the re-formed Hanoverian army.

Former officers of the Legion were asked to supply details of their service in 1828. These records, arranged alphabetically, are in WO 25/749-779. There is an incomplete card index, arranged by name, in the Research Enquiries Room. Some birth, baptism, marriage and death certificates for officers are to be found in WO 42/52-58.

Soldiers' documents for men who served in the Legion are in WO 97/1178-1181. A register of recruits for the Legion, 1803-1808, is in WO 25/3203. Statements taken in June 1806 of the period of service of all NCOs and men serving with the Legion are in WO 25/1100-1114. A list of men discharged from the Legion between 1783 and 1810 is in WO 25/1121.

Casualty returns for the Legion are in WO 25/2272-2288, with indexes in WO 25/2752, 2888-2891. Muster rolls are in WO 12/11747-11948. Muster rolls for artillery units attached to the Legion are in WO 10. Lists of all the men of the Legion present at the Battle of Waterloo are in WO 12/11949. An index to names is available in the Research Enquiries Room.

A register of pensioners from the Legion, 1801-1815, is in WO 23/135. Lists of men discharged to pension in 1816 are in WO 25/3236-3237 and WO 116/25. They give the reason for discharge, age, and place of birth of individuals. An alphabetical list of men in these volumes is kept at Kew. Registers of payments made between 1843 and 1867 to soldiers who had served in the Legion are in PMG 7.

Many records of the Legion are held by the Niedersaechsischen Hauptstaatarchiv, Am Archiv 1, D-3000 Hannover 1, Germany.

13.4 1815-1854

Discharge documents for men who served in the Foreign Veterans Battalion, 1815-1861, are in WO 122, together with reports of medical boards on individuals in these regiments, 1816-1817. A statement of the service by officers in foreign legions from about 1817 is in WO 25/3236-3237.

Registers of half pay given to officers who had served with foreign regiments, 1819-1824, are in WO 24/763-766. Other registers of half pay and pensions to former officers who had served in foreign regiments between 1822 and 1885 are in PMG 6.

13.5 The Crimean War

At the outbreak of the War in 1854 foreign mercenary troops were recruited for service in the Crimea. See C C Bayley, *Mercenaries for the Crimea* (London, 1977). They formed the British German, Swiss, and Italian Legions. Muster rolls, service records and attestation forms for the British German and Swiss Legions are in WO 15 (none have survived for the Italian Legion). At the end of the War the Legions were disbanded and many men emigrated to the Cape of Good Hope. WO 15 also contains a list of officers and men of the British German Legion who settled in the Cape in 1856. The families who emigrated are listed in Esme Bull, *Aided immigration from Britain to South Africa, 1857-1867* (Pretoria, 1990).

Returns of half pay made to officers of foreign regiments between 1858 and 1876 are in WO 23/79-81. Registers of payments to widows of officers between 1855 and 1858 are in WO 23/113, and between 1858 and 1868 in WO 23/88.

13.6 Second World War

A number of Polish soldiers escaped after the collapse of Poland in 1939 and fought in Polish units attached to allied armies during the war. War diaries for some Polish units are in WO 169 and WO 170.

Because of the political situation in Poland many of these soldiers and their families did not wish to return home after the war had ended. A Polish Resettlement Corps was set up in 1946 to ease the transition of Poles to civilian life in Britain and abroad. The records of the Corps are in WO 315 and contain many items of interest to the family historian. A number of the files are in Polish, however, and some have either been retained by the Ministry of Defence or are closed for seventy-five years.

Service records of Free Poles are retained by the Ministry of Defence, CS(R) 2e Polish Branch, Bourne Avenue, Hayes, Middx UB3 1RF. MoD will undertake a search only on receipt of a written request from the next of kin.

14

RECORDS OF ANCILLARY SERVICES

14.1 Barrackmasters

Barrackmasters were responsible for the construction and maintenance of barracks. A separate Barrackmaster General's Department was established under War Office control in 1793. In 1808 the department was transferred to the Treasury, and then in 1822 to the Board of Ordnance. On the transfer of the Board to the War Office in 1855 the department was disbanded.

Barrackmasters are listed in the monthly Army Lists. WO 54 includes appointment papers and testimonials for barrackmasters between 1808 and 1852, and for barrackmaster sergeants, 1823-1855 (WO 54/715-716, 756-823, 928-929). Some papers about the appointment of barrackmasters and their staff between 1835 and 1879 also appear in the registers of the Commissariat Department in WO 61/7-11. Pay and allowance books, 1797-1824, are in WO 54/704-713. Returns of service of barrackmasters in the British Isles, 1830-1852, are in WO 54/734, 742. An alphabetical list of barrackmaster sergeants, 1771-1824, is in WO 54/948.

14.2 Chaplains

Until the end of the eighteenth century chaplains were employed on a regimental and garrison basis. In 1796 a chaplain general was appointed and chaplains were allocated, one to a brigade or to three or four regiments. The first Presbyterian chaplains were appointed in 1827, Roman Catholics in 1836, Wesleyans in 1881, and Jewish chaplains in 1892.

Registers of certificates of service of chaplains, 1817-1843, are in WO 25/256-258. Lists of payments to chaplains, 1805-1842, are in WO 25/233-251. Lists of chaplains receiving retired pay, 1806-1837, are in WO 25/252-253 and many relate to those who saw service in the eighteenth century. Information about the appointment of chaplains and their conditions of pay and service is in the out-letter books of the War Office Accounts Department, 1810-1836, in WO 7/60-65, and in the in-letters of the Chaplain General's Department, 1808-1828, in WO 7/66-72.

Short biographies of chaplains are in *Crockford's Clerical Directory* and the *Catholic Directory*. Chaplains are British army officers and so are included in the Army Lists.

Further records are held by Ministry of Defence Chaplains, Netheravon House, Salisbury Road, Netheravon, Wiltshire SP4 9SY.

14.3 Civilian Employees

Many thousands of men in dozens of different occupations have always been employed to help run the Army. Unfortunately very few records of their employment have survived. Senior civil servants at the War Office are listed in the *Imperial Calendar* and the *War Office List* published between 1861 and 1964. The List often includes brief biographies of certain individuals. It is available in the Research Enquiries Room at Kew.

Registers of pensions and superannuation payable to civilian employees, 1820-1892, are in WO 23/93-104. Pay books, rolls of names and other papers for civilians employed by the War Office between 1803 and 1919 are in WO 25/3957-3991.

Records of the War Office Boy Messenger Friendly Society and War Office School are in WO 371 and WO 32. The Society was set up in 1906 and continued until the outbreak of the First World War in 1914: a list of its members is in WO 371/3.

14.4 Commissariat

The Commissariat Department was responsible for the victualling of the Army and was set up in 1793. Before then a decentralized system of supply by civilian contractors, or the appointment of special Commissary Generals for specific campaigns, provided for the Army's needs. The Colonel and other officers of a regiment would provide their men with food and clothing, the cost of which would be deducted from their wages. Ireland had its own Commissariat Department, the records of which, spanning 1797 to 1852, are in WO 63. In 1816 the Commissariat Department came under the control of the Treasury, but was transferred back to the

War Office in 1854. Treasury Board papers in T 1 and letter books in T 64 may refer to individual Commissariat officers in this period. Commissary officers were normally civilians but were subject to military discipline and wore uniform.

There are registers of full pay, half pay and pensions awarded to Commissary Officers between 1810 and 1856 in WO 61/61-93, with lists of pensions granted to widows, 1814-1826, in WO 61/96-97. Registers of half pay awarded to officers between 1834 and 1885 are in PMG 5. Description and succession books for officers between 1855 and 1869, especially those in the Military Train (which was responsible for supplying the Army while abroad), are in WO 25/580-602, 824. Returns of officers' services for the Military Train in 1868 and 1869 are in WO 25/824/2.

Registers in WO 61/1-16 cover the appointment of men to the department between 1798 and 1889. Establishment lists, in WO 61/25-60, give the names of men employed in Spain and Portugal in 1809, and at various stations at home and abroad between 1816 and 1868. Records of Commissariat establishments in Spain and Portugal, 1810-1813 are in AO 11/20.

Applications for employment as clerks in the Commissariat, 1812-1813, 1825-1854 are in WO 61/104-105. Letters relating to civilian appointments in the Commissariat, 1798-1855, are in WO 58/1-47. Registers of appointments and other papers relating to the employment of civil staff by the Commissariat, 1789-1879, are in WO 61. WO 77 contains the papers of Thomas Archer, a clerk in the Commissariat, covering the period 1814-1838.

14.5 Invalids and Veterans

From the late seventeenth century a number of companies of invalids were formed. They consisted of soldiers partly disabled by wounds, and veterans who, from old age and length of service, had been rendered incapable of the duties of an active campaign, but were able to undertake lighter duties. Invalid companies were engaged in garrison duty both at home and in the colonies. The first companies were raised in 1690. From 1703 responsibility for raising and administering the companies was placed with the Royal Hospital Chelsea and a Royal Corps of Invalids was formed. It was disbanded when invalids fit for service became part of the new Royal Garrison Regiment and the remainder went on to the strength of the newly formed Veteran Battalions. These battalions were used extensively to maintain civil peace at home. Between 1842 and 1846 they were re-formed as the Enrolled Pensioners. In 1867 the Pensioners were merged into the Second Class Army Reserve available for home service.

Description and succession books for officers serving with the Garrison Battalions between 1809 and 1815 are in WO 25/567, 571-573, 578. Other description books for Veteran Battalions between 1813 and 1826 are in WO 25/605-625. Records of officers serving with the Royal Garrison Regiment between 1901 and 1905 are in WO 19.

Soldiers' documents for men serving in Veteran Battalions between 1804 and 1854 are in WO 97. A register of men in the Garrison and Veteran Battalions, 1845-1854, is in WO 23/27. There is a series of certificates of service in Invalid and Veteran Battalions, 1782-1833, in WO 121/137-222. Casualty returns for both the Veteran and Garrison regiments, 1809-1830, are in WO 25/2190-2195, 2216-2243.

Muster returns for companies and battalions are in WO 12. Monthly returns for companies stationed at garrisons, 1759 to 1802, which sometimes include lists of officers, are in WO 17/793-802.

A brief history of the invalids may be found in Michael Mann, 'The Corps of Invalids', *Journal of the Society for Army Historical Research* vol 66, no 1 (1988).

14.6 Medical Services

From 1660, each regiment had a surgeon (commissioned) and each regiment of foot also had a surgeon's mate (warranted). There was also a Surgeon General and a Physician General who were replaced in 1810 by the Army Medical Department. In 1855 NCOs and men serving in hospitals were formed into the Medical Staff Corps, from 1857 the Army Hospital Corps. The regimental system was abolished in 1873 and all medical officers became part of a common Army Medical Department staff. In September 1884 the Department and the Army Hospital Corps were linked together in close association, and they finally merged to form the Royal Army Medical Corps in 1898.

There is a series of records of service of officers of the Medical Department, 1800-1840, in WO 25/3896-3912, which includes details of the professional education of surgeons. Returns of medical staff in Great Britain, 1811-1813, are in WO 25/259-260, with returns of pay, 1813-1818, at home, in the Peninsula and in France in WO 25/261-263. Pay lists for Staff medical officers, clerks and apothecaries, 1799-1847, and regimental surgeons and assistants, 1790-1847, are in WO 25/3897-3902, with an index in WO 25/3903. Service records for officers of the Medical Department between 1800 and 1840 are in WO 25/3904-3911, with an index in WO 25/3912.

They include details of medical education received. Indexed volumes of candidates for commission as surgeons, 1825-1867, are in WO 25/3923-3943. Confidential reports on medical officers in 1860 and 1861 are in WO 25/3944. R Drew's *List of Commissioned Medical Officers of the Army, 1660-1960* (2 vols, 1925, 1968) is available in the Research Enquiries Room.

There are few records of military hospitals and medical units other than for the two world wars. Some returns of patients at Lisbon and Belen, 1812-1813, and in Ordnance hospitals, 1809-1852, are in WO 25/260, 265, and sick returns sent in to the Army Medical departments, 1817-1892, including annual death and disability returns which name individuals, are in WO 334.

Soldiers' documents for the Army Hospital Corps, 1855-1872, are in WO 97/1698 and the Royal Army Medical Corps medal book, 1879-1896, is in WO 25/3992.

Appointment papers for the Ordnance Board Medical Department, 1835-1847, are in WO 54/926. Returns of officers and men serving with the department between 1835 and 1850 are in WO 54/234 and 926.

14.7 Nursing Services

Florence Nightingale's hospital at Scutari during the Crimean War (1854-1856) was the first to use women as nurses for British soldiers. Prior to this nursing duties were carried out by male orderlies seconded by regiments to serve in regimental hospitals.

Six women nurses and a superintendent were employed by the Army Hospital Corps to serve at Woolwich and Netley in 1861. An Army Nursing Service was formed in 1881 and efforts were made to increase the numbers of female nurses in the Army. An Army Nursing Reserve was established in 1897. Both the Reserve and the Service were reorganized after the South African War (1899-1902) as Queen Alexandra's Imperial Military Nursing Service (QAIMNS). The present title of Queen Alexandra's Royal Army Nursing Corps (QARANC) was assumed in 1949.

Testimonials for nurses who wished to serve with Florence Nightingale during the Crimean War are in WO 25/264. Lydia Notley's application to serve as a nurse is illustrated in **figure 19**. She had worked as a nurse in London for fifteen years and was recruited but then discharged as 'considered too stout [to] sustain her health in the East'.

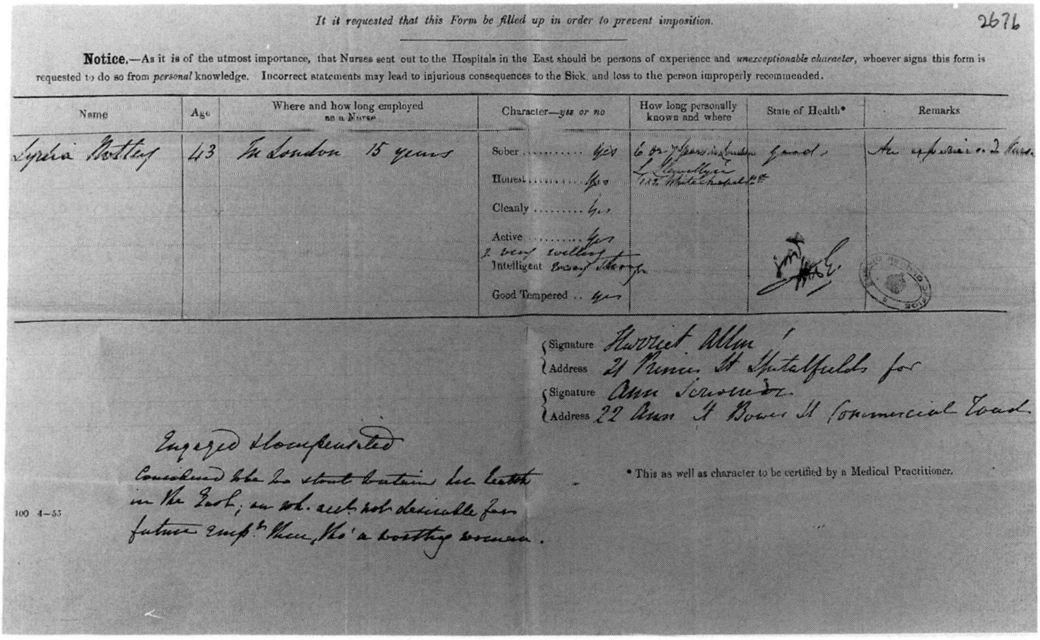

It it requested that this Form be filled up in order to prevent imposition. 2676

Notice.—As it is of the utmost importance, that Nurses sent out to the Hospitals in the East should be persons of experience and *unexceptionable character*, whoever signs this form is requested to do so from *personal* knowledge. Incorrect statements may lead to injurious consequences to the Sick, and loss to the person improperly recommended.

Name	Age	Where and how long employed as a Nurse	Character—*yes or no*	How long personally known and where	State of Health*	Remarks
Lydia Notley	43	In London 15 years	Sober ... yes Honest ... yes Cleanly ... yes Active ... yes Intelligent Good Tempered .. yes	6 or 7 years in London	good	

Signature Harriet Allen

Address 21 Princes St Spitalfields for

Signature Ann Schroeder

Address 22 Ann St Bower St Commercial Road

Engaged & compensated

* This as well as character to be certified by a Medical Practitioner.

100 4—55

Fig 19 Application of Lydia Notley to serve as a nurse, c 1855. (WO 25/264)

Nominal and seniority rolls for nurses in the voluntary National Aid Society and the Army Nursing Service, 1869-1891, are in WO 25/3955. An indexed register of candidates for appointment as staff nurses, 1903-1926, is in WO 25/3956.

Few nurses qualified for a pension because they rarely served enough years to receive one. Pension records for nurses appointed before 1905 are in WO 23/93-95, 181. Registers of pensions for QAIMNS nurses, 1909-1928, are in PMG 34/1-5 and First World War disability pensions for nurses are in PMG 42/1-12.

In 1883 Queen Victoria instituted the Royal Red Cross to be awarded to military nurses. A register for its award from 1883 to 1918 is in WO 145. The Queen's and King's South Africa Medals were awarded to nurses for service during the South African War, 1899-1902; medal rolls are in WO 100.

Record cards for Voluntary Aid Detachment (VAD) nurses during both world wars are held by the British Red Cross Society, Archive Section, Bamett Hill, Wonersh, Guildford, Surrey, GU5 0RF.

14.8 Ordnance Office

The Ordnance Office was run separately from the War Office until 1855. It was responsible for the supply of guns, ammunition and warlike stores to the Army. It also controlled the Royal Artillery and the Royal Engineers. A brief administrative history of the Office is in the PRO *Guide* Part 1, section 705 and Michael Roper's *Records of the War Office*. Records relating to the Royal Artillery and the Royal Engineers are described in chapters 5 and 6 respectively.

Registers of employees of the Board of Ordnance, 1811-1847, are in WO 54/511-671. Appointment papers for barrackmasters, clerks and other people employed by the Board between 1819 and 1855 are in WO 54/756-903, 927. Miscellaneous correspondence relating to people employed by the Office is in WO 44/695-700.

Registers of Ordnance pensions being paid in 1834, when responsibility was transferred to the Royal Hospital Chelsea, are in WO 23/141-145.

The monthly Orders of the Army Ordnance Corps, 1901-1919, are in WO 111. These include a great deal about promotions, awards, deaths, discharges and courts martial.

14.9 Ordnance Survey

Between 1790 and 1805, map-making was carried out by civilians working under the direction of Royal Engineer officers. In 1805 the civilians were formed into the Corps of Military Surveyors and Draughtsmen. The Corps was disbanded in 1817 and the previous system reinstated. A card index containing the names of men who served either in the Corps or as civilians is held by the PRO Map Department at Kew. The index is based on information in WO 54/208 and other documents, and contains details of appointments and promotions. From 1824 a number of survey companies, initially from the Royal Corps of Sappers and Miners and later from the Royal Engineers, were set up to help with the work of the Survey. The records of these men can be found in exactly the same way as those of other servicemen.

A list of Royal Engineer officers who served in the Survey between 1791 and 1927 is in OS 1/1. A register of soldiers who died while serving with 13 Survey Company between 1829 and 1859 is in OS 3/300. This gives information about the cause of death and disposal of personal effects. OS 1/1/4 contains a list of all Royal Engineers serving with the Survey on 1 July 1890. A register of marriages of men in 16 Survey

Company between 1901 and 1929, together with the birth dates of any children, is in OS 3/341. OS 3/275-277 contains seniority lists between 1935 and 1942.

14.10 Royal Marines

Marines were raised in 1664 as land soldiers to serve on ships. Royal Marines were never under the control of the Army, but were always the responsibility of the Royal Navy. As a result there are very few records relating to the Marines in War Office classes. Marine records of interest to genealogists in Admiralty (ADM) classes are fully described in Garth Thomas's *Records of the Royal Marines* (PRO Readers' Guide No 10, 1994).

14.11 Schools and Colleges

The Duke of York's Royal Military School was founded in 1802 as The Royal Military Asylum for Children of Soldiers of the Regular Army at Chelsea, moving to Dover in 1909. It assumed its present name in 1892. Admission and discharge books for children from 1803 to 1923 are in WO 143/17-25, with an index of admissions, 1910-1958, in WO 143/26. An apprenticeship book for the period 1806 to 1848 is in WO 143/52. Summaries of offences committed by boys, 1852-1879, are in WO 143/53-58. A record of admissions to the School, 1906-1956, is in WO 143/70. Girls were admitted to the female branch until 1840 but this was abolished in 1846.

At first many of the children were not orphans, but most later entrants appear to have lost at least their father and quite frequently both parents. Children appear to have been admitted between the ages of two and ten, and were discharged in their mid-teens. Most of the girls not claimed by their parents were apprenticed, often as servants: the boys went into the Army, or were apprenticed if they were not fit for military service. The admission and discharge registers, 1803-1923, are very informative: they are arranged by date of admission (WO 143/17-26), although one of the boys' registers, for 1804-1820, is in alphabetical order. The information for the girls is the fuller: number, name, age, date of admission, from what regiment, rank of father (P, T, S, etc, for private, trooper, sergeant), parents' names and, if living, parochial settlement, when dismissed, and how disposed of (eg died, retained by parents while on pass, apprenticed). The boys' admission register gives the same information with the exception of parents' names. The discharge registers give more information on the child's future - apprenticeship, service in a regiment, etc.

A similar school, the Royal Hibernian Military School, was set up in Ireland in 1769. It was amalgamated with the Duke of York's School in 1924. Many of its records were destroyed by enemy action in 1940. An index of admissions to the School drawn up in 1863, with retrospective entries to c 1835 and annotations to approximately 1919, is in WO 143/27.

Records of the Royal Military Academy, Woolwich established in 1741 to train engineer and artillery officers, and the Royal Military College, which was founded in 1799 to train cadets and regimental officers (WO 99, WO 149 - WO 151, WO 314), are available to the public at Sandhurst where the two institutions were merged in 1947. They may be consulted by arrangement with the Commandment.

14.12 Military Intelligence and Special Operations

An Intelligence Branch was established by the War Office in 1873 becoming the Military Intelligence Division in 1887 and Directorate of Military Operations in 1904. Intelligence papers from earlier periods may also survive, eg the Scovell Papers (WO 37) contain intercepted correspondence and intelligence papers collected by General Scovell as Commander of the Corps of Guides and chief cypher officer in the Peninsular War, and are more fully described in Michael Roper's *Records of the War Office*.

A Secret Service Bureau was established in 1909 and records of the counter-intelligence service, which subsequently became MI5, covering the period 1909-1919, are now available in the record class KV 1. These include accounts of payments to members of staff in KV 1/11-12, 69-70 and lists of staff in KV 1/52, 59. Many of its wartime employees were women. These records have been published on CD-ROM - *MI5: The First Ten Years* (PRO, 1998).

Recently released records of the Special Operations Executive (SOE) are in the record classes HS 1-HS 6 and many contain detailed information on operations carried out by army personnel and foreign nationals serving with SOE. Further information about these records may be found in John Cantwell's *The Second World War. A Guide to Sources* (PRO Handbook No 15, 1998 revised edition).

15

PRISONERS OF WAR

15.1 Introduction

There are few records for men in the British Army who were prisoners before 1914. WO 40/2 contains a list of British and American Prisoners of War (PoWs) drawn up in 1781 with a view to exchange. Other lists are in T 64. Lists and accounts of British PoWs in France and elsewhere for the period between 1793 and 1814, transmitted by the agent for prisoners in Paris, are among the registers of PoWs in ADM 103. They appear, however, to cover largely naval and civilian internees. A list of PoWs at Valenciennes between 1805 and 1813 is in WO 25/2409.

British PoWs taken in the Crimea and by the Boers between 1899 and 1902 are listed in the *London Gazette*, but these lists are incomplete and generally name only officers, arranged under regiments. The South African Field Force Casualty Roll, 1899-1902, lists the names and regiments of men captured by the Boers.

15.2 First World War

AIR 1/892 contains lists of British and dominion PoWs held in Germany, Turkey and Switzerland in 1916. A list of British and Dominion army PoWs in German camps, especially the one at Giessen, in July 1915 is in ADM 1/8420/124. Interviews and reports of the Committee on the Treatment of British Prisoners of War between 1915 and 1919 are in WO 161/95-101. They are closed for seventy-five years. There is a substantial amount about PoWs in the General Correspondence of the Foreign Office (FO 371) and a specific class of records dealing with PoWs (FO 383), although few files relating to individuals survive. Deaths while a prisoner are recorded in registers held at the Family Records Centre.

A list of officer PoWs was compiled by the military agents Cox and Co in 1919 called a *List of Officers taken prisoner in the various Theatres of War between August 1914 and November 1918*. It was reprinted in 1988 and is available in the Research Enquiries Room.

Army officers captured during the First World War had to submit a report on the circumstances of their capture, when they were repatriated at the end of the war. Many of these reports can be found in their records of service. For further details see section 16.2.2.

15.3 Second World War

WO 392 contains lists of all British and Dominions PoWs held by the Germans and Italians from 1939 to 1945, including the Merchant Navy. A series of three volumes, entitled *Prisoners of War*, containing the names and service details of 169,000 British and Dominions PoWs in German hands on 30 March 1945, can be consulted in the Research Enquiries Room.

Information concerning PoWs in Japanese hands is more comprehensive than that for PoWs held by the Germans and Italians. The main source is the card index WO 345. This consists of 57,000 cards of Allied PoWs and civilian internees, arranged alphabetically. Registers of Allied PoWs and civilians held in camps in Singapore can be found in WO 367. WO 347 consists of the hospital records for Allied PoWs held in Asia. A further alphabetical list of British PoWs in Japan and Japanese occupied territory can be found in WO 392/23-26, while other nominal lists are in FO 916 and CO 980. Escape and Evasion Reports for the Far East can be found in AIR 40/2462 and WO 208/3493-3494. The Interrogation Reports of liberated PoWs from the Far East are in WO 203/5193-5199, 5640 and WO 208/3499.

Information about individuals may occasionally be found among War Office files in WO 32 (code 91), and WO 219/1402, 1448-1474. The War Diary of MI9, the division of Military Intelligence which dealt with escaped prisoners of all services, is in WO 165/39, and its papers are in WO 208. Medical reports on conditions in PoW camps, with some reports on escapes, are among the Medical Historians Papers in WO 222/1352-1393. Further reports and lists of men sometimes occur in the Judge Advocate General's war crimes papers in WO 235, WO 309, WO 310, WO 311, WO 325, WO 331, WO 344, WO 356 and WO 367.

The International Committee of the Red Cross in Geneva keeps lists of all known PoWs and internees of all nationalities for both World Wars. Searches are only made in response to written requests and an hourly fee is charged. Contact the International Council of the Red Cross, Archives Division, 19 Avenue de la Paix, CH-1202, Geneva, Switzerland. Enquiries within the United Kingdom concerning these lists should be sent to: The Director, International Welfare Department, British Red Cross Society, 9 Grosvenor Crescent, London SW1X 7EJ.

15.4 Korea

Lists of British and Commonwealth PoWs of all services, between January 1951 and July 1953, are in WO 208/3999. The Historical Records and Reports on the Korean War in WO 308/54 also contain a list of Commonwealth prisoners compiled in January 1954. General correspondence covering PoWs is in WO 162/208-264, WO 32/19273 and DO 35/5853-5863.

16

FIRST WORLD WAR

16.1 Introduction

The best introduction to records in the Public Record Office relating to an individual's service in World War I is *Army Service records of the First World War* by Simon Fowler, William Spencer and Stuart Tamblin (PRO Readers Guide No 19, revised edition, 1997). This includes illustrations of the types of document you are likely to find, which include attestation papers, discharge papers, medical records and casualty forms. You may also find useful Norman Holding, *World War I Army Ancestry* (FFHS, 1997). He has also written *More Sources of World War I Army Ancestry* (FFHS, 1991) and *The Location of British Army records: a National Directory of World War I Sources* (FFHS, 1991).

Victor Neuburg, *A guide to the Western Front: A companion for Travellers* (London, 1988) is both a valuable introduction to the organization of the Army and a guide to the battlefields of Flanders and France during the First World War. An interesting account of life in the trenches is in Dennis Winter, *Death's men* (London, 1978).

16.2 Service Records

16.2.1 Other ranks

We do not know how many men served as other ranks during the First World War as most of their service records were destroyed by bombing in 1940, but records relating to c 2.75 million men do survive. Those described here only relate to men who were discharged or died between 1914 and 1920. They may include records relating to regular soldiers who first joined the army in the late nineteenth century, but they will not contain the records of those who continued to serve after 1920 or who transferred to one of the other services, taking their service record with them. It has been estimated that you have about a 40 per cent chance of finding the service records of a particular soldier who served in the First World War.

To find a surviving service record, it is useful to know the man's full name, his rank, service number and regiment. If you do not have this information, you can get it from the First World War Medal Index cards described in section 16.5. Bear in mind that he may have served in more than one regiment and had more than one service number and that there may be several individuals with exactly the same forenames and surnames.

The surviving First World War service records are preserved in two record classes, both of which are available only on microfilm.

The records in WO 364, sometimes known as the 'Unburnt Records', are a collection of some 750,000 individual records of service, primarily for men who were discharged as a result of sickness or wounds contracted or received during the war. All of this class is now available. If your soldier survived and received a pension, start with WO 364. Alphabetically arranged, they relate to those discharged on medical or other grounds and regular soldiers who were discharged at the end of their period of service and were awarded a pension. Men who had signed up for the duration normally only received a gratuity on demobilization, not a pension, unless they were awarded one on medical grounds.

The records of approximately 2,000,000 individuals are being transferred into the record class WO 363. They are being microfilmed in random letter blocks, funded by generous grants from the Heritage Lottery Fund, and filming will not be completed until 2003. At the time of writing (August 1998) only surnames beginning with the letters E, N, O, Q, U, V and Z are available. The class is arranged by first letter of surname, but after that it is not in a proper alphabetical order. The records in WO 363 include men who completed their service as well as those who were killed or who died of wounds, or were executed.

16.2.2 Officers

The records of service of some 217, 000 officers who saw service during the First World War, were released in February 1998. The records released include all branches of the army, including the Royal Flying Corps, and are in the record classes WO 339 (with an index in WO 338) and WO 374.

WO 374 is the smaller class, containing some 77,800 records, and mostly relates to those who were commissioned into the Territorial Army or had a temporary commission. It is arranged alphabetically and the class list gives a full list of names.

WO 339 contains the service records of over 140,000 officers, arranged by 'long number'. You must identify this 'long number' by using the alphabetical index of names in WO 338, which is seen on microfilm. Service records should be found here if the officer ceased serving before 1922 and was a pre-war regular officer, was commissioned into the Special Reserve of officers or was given an Emergency Commission in the regular army. The service records of a few notable individuals, such as Wilfred Owen, are in WO 138.

For further information about the records described in sections 16.2.1 and 16.2.2, together with details about other records relating to the First World War, see section 3.6.3 and *Army Service Records of the First World War*.

16.2.3 Records of service after 1920

The records of those men, both officers and other ranks who saw service after 1920 (other ranks) and 1922 (officers) are still maintained by the Ministry of Defence at CS(R)2b, Bourne Avenue, Hayes, Middlesex, UB3 1RF. The MoD will only carry out searches for next of kin on payment of a £25 fee.

16.3 Casualty Records

A list of men, arranged by regiment, who died during the war was published in *Soldiers who died in the Great War* (80 vols, HMSO, 1921). There is a similar volume for officers who died during the war. Microfilmed copies of these publications are kept in the Microfilm Reading Room. Another good source for officers is *Cross of Sacrifice* by S and B Jarvis (1993) which covers all the armed services.

A roll of honour for men of the London Stock Exchange who served in the forces is kept in the Research Enquiries Room. Lists of employees of the Midland Railway who were either wounded or killed in action are in RAIL 491/1259. A similar roll of honour for men of the London, Brighton and South Coast Railway is in RAIL 414/761 and for the North Eastern Railway in RAIL 527/993.

French and Belgian death certificates for British soldiers who died in hospitals or elsewhere outside the immediate war zone between 1914 and 1920 are in RG 35/45-69. They are arranged by first letter of surname and can be informative, but are in French or Flemish.

A list of men killed or wounded during the Easter Rising in Dublin in 1916 is in WO 35/69.

The Commonwealth War Graves Commission records all soldiers who died, or who were reported missing in action, during the war. Their records indicate the unit with which the soldier was serving and his place of burial. Their address is: Commonwealth War Graves Commission, 2 Marlow Road, Maidenhead SL6 7DX.

16.4 Medical and Disability Records

A selection of case files, covering a cross-section of disability pensions awarded after the First World War, is in PIN 26, but they are closed to public inspection for fifty years. MH 106 contains a specimen collection of admission and discharge registers from hospitals, casualty clearing stations and the like. The class also contains some medical cards for individuals, including the Queen Mary's Auxiliary Army Corps (see section 16.9).

Ledgers of the payment of disability retired pay during and after the First World War are in PMG 42. Ledgers for supplementary allowances and special grants to officers, their widows and dependents are in PMG 43. Those for pensions to relatives of deceased officers are in PMG 44, widows' pensions in PMG 45, children's allowances in PMG 46, and pay to relatives of missing officers in PMG 47.

16.5 Medal Rolls

Copies of rolls of awards of the British War Medal, Victory Medal, 1914 Star, 1914-1915 Star, Territorial Force War Medal, and Silver War Badge are in WO 329. They are awards to officers and other ranks of the Army, including nurses, and to the Royal Flying Corps. There is a card index in the record class WO 372, which is seen on microfiche in the Microfilm Reading Room. It covers all those who received these medals, arranged by name. The rolls themselves give the unit the man served in, his service number, the theatres of war he served in, and the medals to which he was entitled. In most cases the card index contains as much information as the medal roll.

Card indexes are also available in the Microfilm Reading Room to recipients of the following gallantry medals: Distinguished Conduct Medal, Meritorious Service Medal, and Military Medal, and to individuals mentioned in despatches. The cards give a reference to the *London Gazette* in which the award was gazetted. Sometimes a full citation was printed in the *Gazette* for the Distinguished Conduct Medal. Very occasionally a citation is given in full for the award of the Military Medal. Copies of the *London Gazette* are in ZJ 1.

Supplements to the Monthly Army Lists contain lists of recipients of medals but give no date or reason for the award. Lists of foreign awards to individuals are also included. Some records of these awards are in FO 371 and FO 372. Complete lists of all recipients of medals are given in the Supplements to the Monthly Army Lists during 1919.

16.6 War Diaries

From 1907 units on active service were required by the Field Service Regulations to keep a daily record of events. These records were called War Diaries or, occasionally, Intelligence Summaries. The diaries contain daily reports on operations, intelligence reports and other pertinent material. A substantial number of maps, once included in these diaries, have been extracted and are now in WO 153. Many diaries are difficult to read because they were often scribbled in pencil in haste, using abbreviations which are now difficult to decipher, or they may be the third copy of a triplicate. Examples of war diaries, service records, aerial photographs and trench maps have been reproduced in two document packs published by the Public Record Office - *Battlefront: 1st July 1916. The first day of the Somme* (PRO, 1998) and *Battlefront: 6th November 1917. The fall of Passchendaele (PRO, 1997)*.

Most war diaries are in WO 95. Certain diaries containing particularly confidential material are in WO 154. They are closed for seventy-five years. Access is permitted provided that an undertaking not to reveal details of a personal nature is signed. These undertaking forms are available at the Research Enquiries Room desk.

The diaries are those of British and colonial units serving in theatres of operations between 1914 and 1922, principally France and Flanders, but also Italy, Mesopotamia, Palestine, Salonika, Russia, home and colonial forces, and of the post-war armies of occupation. They are arranged by theatre of operations and then by army, corps and division.

Provided that the unit is known, these war diaries can be a useful way of fleshing out the career of a man during the war. It is unusual, however, for a war diary to mention individuals, unless they are officers or NCOs. The example illustrated as **figure 20** records the death in action of Lt Colonel Holberton. Periods of combat are also likely to be described only in brief, and deaths of men or examples of gallantry may not be mentioned. Where a unit served can be traced through the Orders of Battle in WO 95/5467-5493 or by consulting the published Order of Battle by Becke, which is available in the Research Enquiries Room.

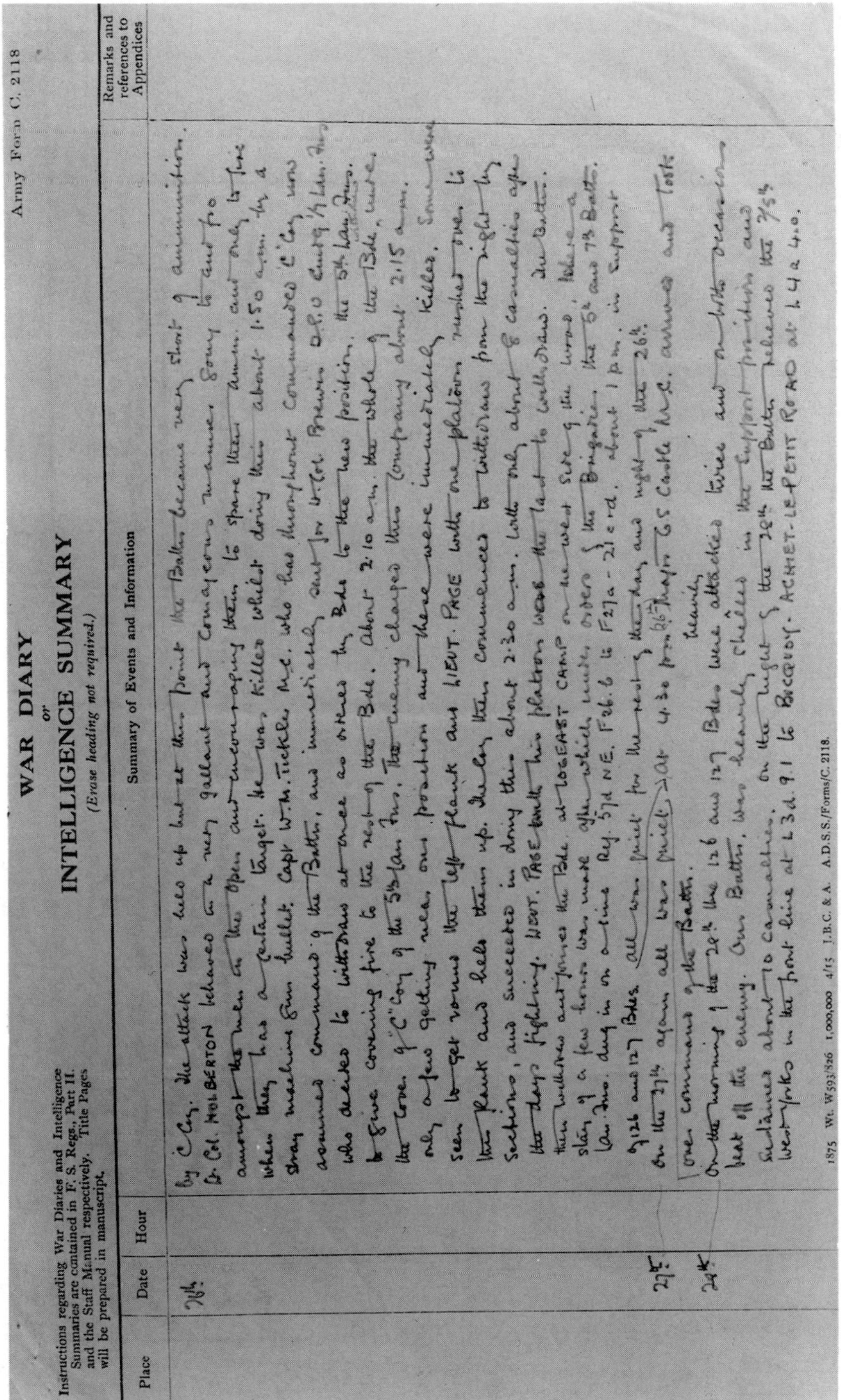

Army Form C. 2118

Instructions regarding War Diaries and Intelligence Summaries are contained in F. S. Regs., Part II. and the Staff Manual respectively. Title Pages will be prepared in manuscript.

WAR DIARY
or
INTELLIGENCE SUMMARY
(Erase heading not required.)

Place	Date	Hour	Summary of Events and Information	Remarks and references to Appendices
	26th		by C Coy. The attack was held up but at this point the Battn. became very short of ammunition. Lt. Col. HOLBERTON behaved in a very gallant and courageous manner, going to and fro amongst the men in the open and encouraging them, to spare their ammn. and only to fire when they had a certain target. He was killed whilst doing this about 1.50 a.m. by a stray machine gun bullet. Capt W.M. Tickle M.C. who had throughout commanded 'C' Coy now assumed command of the Battn. and immediately sent for Lt. Col. Brewis D.S.O. [illegible] who decided to withdraw at once as ordered by Bde to the new position, the 5th Lan. Fus. to give covering fire to the rest of the Bde. About 2.10 a.m. the whole of the Bde. [illegible] the Coy. of the 5th Lan. Fus. The enemy charged this Company about 2.15 a.m. only a few getting near our position and these were immediately killed. Some were seen to get round the left flank and LIEUT. PAGE with one platoon rushed over to the flank and held them up. The Coy then commenced to withdraw from the right by sections, and succeeded in doing this about 2.30 a.m. with only about 8 casualties after the days fighting. LIEUT. PAGE brought his platoon [illegible] the last to withdraw. The Battn. then withdrew and joined the Bde. at LOGEAST CAMP on the west side of the wood. Here a stay of a few hours was made after which, under orders of the Brigadier, the 5th and 7th Battns. Lan. Fus. dug in on a line Ref. 57d NE. F26.b to F27a - 21 c r d. about 1 p.m. in support of 126 and 127 Bdes. All was quiet for the rest of the day and night of the 26th.	
	27th		On the 27th again all was quiet. At 4.30 p.m. [illegible] Major G.S. Castle M.C. arrived and took over command of the Battn.	
	28th		On the morning of the 28th the 126 and 127 Bdes. were attacked twice and on both occasions beat off the enemy. Our Battn. was heavily shelled in the support position and sustained about 10 casualties. On the night of the 28th the Battn. relieved the [illegible] in the front line at L 3 d. 9.1 to BUCQUOY - ACHIET-LE-PETIT ROAD at L 4 a 4.0.	

1875 Wt. W593/826 1,000,000 4/15 J.B.C. & A. A.D.S.S./Forms/C. 2118.

Fig 20 War Diary of the 5th Battalion, 5th Lancashire Regiment, 26 March 1918. (WO 95/2654)

16.7 Royal Flying Corps

From 1914 until the creation of the Royal Air Force on 1 April 1918 the Royal Flying Corps (RFC), which had been established in 1912, was part of the Army. Many men were recruited into the RFC from other parts of the Army. A selection of RFC squadron, and other unit, records is in AIR 1. They can contain a great deal of valuable information about individuals, especially officers and aircrew, but only a relatively small number survive.

The records of service of RFC airmen with service numbers 329, 000 or lower can be found in AIR 79. If they went on to see service in the Second World War, their records are still held by the RAF at RAF Innsworth, Gloucester GL3 1EZ.

Records of RFC officers can be found in WO 339 and WO 374; see section 16.2.2 for further details. Records of RFC officers who went into the RAF and who did not see service after 1922 can be found in the class AIR 76, which is available in the Microfilm Reading Room.

Records of RFC units and formations will also be found in AIR 23, AIR 25 and AIR 27-AIR 29, with a small selection of early flying log books in AIR 4.

There is a muster roll of other ranks serving in the RFC on 1 April 1918 in AIR 1/ 819. Another copy is in AIR 10/232-237. There are several series of casualty reports from the Western Front for the period April 1916 to November 1918 in AIR 1/843-860, 914-916 and 960-969. Medals awarded to RFC personnel are in WO 329. For further details see section 16.5. Officers are also listed in the Army Lists.

Casualty record cards for men of the RFC, killed or wounded during the war, are held by the RAF Museum, Hendon, London NW9 5LL.

16.8 Conscientious Objectors

After the introduction of conscription in 1915-1916 men could appeal against army service through the Military Service Tribunals. Most records of these tribunals were destroyed after the war. Records for the Middlesex Service Tribunal were preserved, however, and now are in MH 47, and records of a few other Tribunals are held at local record offices.

16.9 Women in the War

As the war progressed, women came to do a number of the jobs previously done by men, such as driving, although they did not take part in actual combat. Correspondence about the employment of women in the Army is to be found in WO 32 (code 68) and WO 162/30-73. These papers contain very little of a genealogical nature.

The Women's Army Auxiliary Corps (WAAC) was formed in 1917 and became the Queen Mary's Auxiliary Army Corps in May 1918. An incomplete nominal roll for the Corps is in WO 162/16. A list of women motor drivers employed in the Women's Army Auxiliary Corps during the war is in WO 162/62. Recommendations for honours are in WO 162/65. War diaries for the Corps in France between 1917 and 1919 are in WO 95/84-85. The records of service of members of the WAAC are on microfilm in the record class WO 398.

Many women served as nurses or otherwise helped in hospitals or elsewhere in the medical services. Records of nurses are described in section 14.7 above. Lists of nurses arriving in France during the war are given in WO 95/3982. Nurses records of service from the First World War will be released in June 1999.

Some medical sheets for members of the Voluntary Aid Detachment and Queen Mary's Auxiliary Ambulance Corps during the First World War are in MH 106/ 2207-2211. Registers of disability and retired pay between 1917 and 1919 are in PMG 42/1-12.

17

SECOND WORLD WAR

17.1 Service Records

Second World War Army service records are still held by the MoD at CS(R)2b, Bourne Avenue, Hayes, Middlesex, UB3 1RF, and as such are not yet at the Public Record Office. Information can only be made available to next of kin on payment of a £25 fee.

17.2 Casualty Returns

Retrospective registers of deaths from enemy action in the Far East between 1941 and 1945 are in RG 33/11, 132, with an index in RG 43/14. A roll of honour for men and women who died during the war is in WO 304.

The Commonwealth War Graves Commission records all soldiers who died, or who were reported missing in action, during the Second World War, as for the First. For details see section 16.3.

17.3 War Diaries

These usually give a much fuller description of the units' activities than their counterparts of the First World War. They often include a detailed narrative of the operations of the unit, together with daily orders, maps and other miscellaneous material. It is unusual for the diaries to contain details about the deaths of, or acts of bravery by, individual men especially those serving in the ranks. Lists of officers are sometimes included.

Most war diaries are closed for one hundred years, but special permission can be obtained to see them by signing an undertaking agreeing not to disclose items relating to individuals. Undertaking forms are obtained from the Research Enquiries Room desk. The war diaries are arranged as follows:

Theatre of operation/force	Class
British Expeditionary Force (France,1939-1940)	WO 167
Central Mediterranean Forces (Italy and Greece, 1943-1946)	WO 170
Dominion Forces	WO 179
GHQ Liaison Regiment	WO 215
Home Forces	WO 166
Madagascar	WO 174
Medical services (ie hospitals, field ambulances etc)	WO 177
Middle East Forces (Egypt, Libya, invasion of Sicily and Italy)	WO 169
Military missions	WO 178
North Africa (Tunisia and Algeria, 1941-1943)	WO 175
North West Expeditionary Force (Norway, 1940)	WO 168
North West Europe (France, Belgium, Holland and Germany, 1944-1946)	WO 171
South-East Asia (India, Burma, Malaya)	WO 172
Special Services	WO 218
Various smaller theatres	WO 176
War Office Directorates	WO 165
West Africa	WO 173

Orders of Battle in WO 212 show where units served. A published copy is available at the Research Enquiries Room desk.

17.4 Home Guard

The PRO holds few papers about the Home Guard, or Local Defence Volunteers as it was first known. A list of Home Guard officers compiled in 1944 is in WO 199/ 3212-3217. WO 199 also contains other records about the Home Guard. WO 900/ 49 contains a sample Home Guard daily report book. Most surviving records are held by local record offices.

Attestation papers, Army Form W 3066, for the Home Guard are held by the Army Medal Office, Government Buildings, Worcester Road, Droitwich, Worcs WR9 8AU. The Office will release information only to next of kin, and can help only if the battalion of the person sought is given.

A *Home Guard List* similar to the Army List is held in the library. L B Whittaker has recently compiled *Stand down: Orders of battle for the units of the Home Guard of the United Kingdom, November 1944* (Newport, Gwent, 1990), which may be of use in tracing units.

17.5 Medals

No medal rolls for the Second World War have yet been transferred to the Public Record Office. They are held by the Army Medal Office, Droitwich (address above). Citations for the Victoria Cross are in CAB 106/312. Citations for awards of gallantry and distinguished service medals are in WO 373. Citations were sometimes published in the *London Gazette,* copies of which are in ZJ 1. See also section 9.2.

17.6 Women in the War

As in the First World War women played a major role in the Army, undertaking many duties which would normally be done by men. Correspondence about the employment of women in the Army is to be found in WO 32 (code 68) and WO 162/30-73. These papers contain very little of a genealogical nature.

Some women served in the Auxiliary Territorial Service (ATS). A few war diaries for the ATS are to be found in WO 166.

Many women served as nurses during the war. War diaries for hospitals and medical units are in WO 177. Each unit also submitted reports, usually of a technical nature, to the War Office. These are in WO 222.

18

OTHER TWENTIETH CENTURY CAMPAIGNS AND THE PEACETIME ARMY

18.1 War Diaries

Apart from the two world wars, the British Army has taken part in a number of operations during this century. The main source of interest for family historians will be the war diaries of participating units. References are:

Campaign	Class
Abyssinia (1935-1936)	WO 191
Egypt (1935-1936)	WO 191
India (1930-1937)	WO 191
Korea (1950-1953)	WO 281
Palestine (1936-1938, 1945-1948)	WO 191
Shanghai (1927-1932)	WO 191
Suez (1956)	WO 288

18.2 Quarterly Historical Reports

Between 1946 and 1950, army units compiled Quarterly Historical Reports. They are similar in format to war diaries, but are not as detailed. The references are:

Area	Class
British Army of the Rhine	WO 267
British Element Trieste Force	WO 264

British Troops Austria	WO 263
Caribbean	WO 270
Central Mediterranean Forces	WO 262
East and West Africa	WO 269
Far East	WO 268
Gibraltar	WO 266
Home Forces	WO 271
Malta	WO 265
Middle East (including Palestine)	WO 261

Quarterly Historical Reports were replaced by the Unit Historical Record in 1950; these are in WO 305. Operation Record Books for the Army Air Corps from 1957 are in WO 295.

19

GENERAL GENEALOGICAL RECORDS

19.1 Registers of Births, Marriages and Deaths

The PRO holds a small number of regimental registers of births, baptisms, marriages and burials. Some of these were annotated with information on discharge: others have baptismal entries for children entered on the same page as the marriage certificate of the parents.

The vast majority of records of births, marriages and deaths after 1837, however, are held by the Office for National Statistics (ONS) and indexes may be consulted at the Family Records Centre. Civil registration records sometimes identify a soldier's regiment, eg the registers of deaths in the Boer War and two World Wars. A summary of the holdings is given in appendix 4.

Registers exist in the PRO for:

3rd battalion King's Own Yorkshire Light Infantry (formerly 1st West Yorkshire Militia): baptisms and marriages, 1865-1904 (WO 68/499/1).

6th battalion, Rifle Brigade (formerly 114th Westmeath Militia): baptisms and marriages, 1834-1904 (WO 68/439).

Royal Artillery: marriages and baptisms, 1817-1827, 1860-1877 (WO 69/551-582).

Royal Horse Artillery: baptisms and marriages, 1859-1877 (WO 69/63-73).

3rd and 4th battalions Somerset Light Infantry (formerly Somerset Militia): baptisms and marriages, 1836-1887, 1892-1903 (WO 68/441).

3rd battalion West Norfolk Regiment: baptisms and marriages, 1863-1908 (WO 68/497).

3rd battalion West Yorkshire Rifles (formerly 2nd West Yorkshire Militia): baptisms and marriages, 1832-1877 (WO 68/499).

In addition, there are registers of births at Dover Castle, 1865-1916 and 1929-1940; Shorncliffe and Hythe, 1878-1939; Buttervant, 1917-1922; and Fermoy, 1920-1921, in WO 156. WO 256 includes burial registers for the Canterbury garrison, 1808-1811, 1859-1884 and 1957-1958; and baptisms and banns of marriage for Army personnel in Palestine, 1939-1947.

Registers of baptisms, 1691-1812, marriages, 1691-1765, and burials, 1692-1856, for the Royal Hospital Chelsea are in RG 4/4330-4332, 4387.

During the eighteenth and early part of the nineteenth centuries applicants for government jobs, including the Army, had to supply a certificate showing their place and date of baptism in order to prove their adherence to the Church of England. A collection of these certificates for officers, extracted from other papers, and dating between 1777 and 1892, is in WO 32/8903-8920 under code 21A. Each piece is indexed. Similar series of certificates, again for officers only, of births, baptisms, marriages, deaths and burials, 1755-1908, extracted from War Office papers and files, is in WO 42; a name index is at the beginning of the class list.

Notifications to the War Office of marriages by officers, 1799-1882, are in WO 25/3239-3245.

19.2 The Census

Apart from 1941, population censuses have been taken every ten years since 1801, but few returns relating to individuals survive before 1841. Census returns for England, Wales, the Isle of Man, and the Channel Islands for 1841 (HO 107), 1851 (HO 107), 1861 (RG 9), 1871 (RG 10), 1881 (RG 11) and 1891 (RG 12) are at the Family Records Centre. Census returns for 1901 (RG 13) will be released in 2002.

Census records for Scotland are held at the General Register Office for Scotland, New Register House, Edinburgh EH1 3YT.

The records include returns for all officers, soldiers, and their families living in barracks or other military establishments on census night, normally the first Sunday in April. The returns give details of where a person was born, marital state, age and occupation. The entire 1881 census has been indexed by name and some indexes of names in particular registration districts have been compiled for other years, notably for 1851.

Census records listing the birthplaces of a soldier's children may thereby tell you where he was stationed earlier in his career. By searching sources that give the location of units, such as the Monthly Returns which are described in section 1.6, you may be able to narrow down the number of regiments that your man may have belonged to, eg if a child is recorded as having been born at Gibraltar in 1850, there may have only been four or five regiments stationed there in that year and so his father is likely to have served with one of those regiments.

A more detailed guide, designed for the family historian, is Susan Lumas's *Making use of the Census* (PRO Readers' Guide No 1, revised edition, 1997).

19.3 Wills

Wills of many men are in the casualty returns in WO 25, with a few wills for officers in WO 42. Wills for soldiers who died abroad, before 1858, may be with the records of the Prerogative Court of Canterbury (PCC). Indexes and registered copies of PCC wills may be seen at the Family Records Centre. Further details are given in PRO Records Information Leaflet 31, *Probate Records* and Miriam Scott's *Prerogative Court of Canterbury Wills and Other Probate Records* (PRO Readers' Guide No 15, 1997).

Copies of wills after 1858 are at the Principal Registry of the Family Division, First Avenue House, High Holborn WC1V 6NP.

APPENDIX 1

Organization Chart of the Army

This chart gives a very brief guide to the organization of the Army as it was between 1881 and 1945.

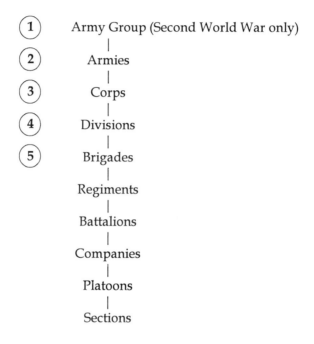

1 Army Group (Second World War only)
|
2 Armies
|
3 Corps
|
4 Divisions
|
5 Brigades
|
Regiments
|
Battalions
|
Companies
|
Platoons
|
Sections

1   Army Group numbers should always be in Arabic numbers. The 21st Army Group (WW2) consisted of the 2nd British Army and the 1st Canadian Army.
2   Army numbers should be in Arabic numbers, eg 2nd Army.
3   Corps are always listed in Roman numerals, eg III Corps.
4   Divisions are always listed with Arabic numbers, sometimes with a regional title, eg 51st (Highland) Division.
5   Brigades are always listed with Arabic numbers, eg 158th Brigade.

During the First World War an Army could consist of two or three Corps; a Corps could consist of up to five Divisions; a Division usually consisted of three Brigades; a Brigade consisted of four Battalions of Infantry until early 1918 and only three Battalions at the end of the war.

APPENDIX 2

Ranks of the British Army

(1) Commissioned Officers

Field Marshal
General
Lieutenant General
Major General
Brigadier
Colonel
Lieutenant Colonel
Major
Captain
Lieutenant
2nd Lieutenant

(2) Non-commissioned officers and other ranks

Warrant Officer 1st Class
Warrant Officer 2nd Class
Sergeant Major
Staff Sergeant
Sergeant
Corporal
Lance Corporal
Private

1 2nd Lieutenant replaced the ranks of Ensign (Infantry) and Cornet (Cavalry) in the mid 19th century.
2 Some ranks used by the army can be deceptive. Corporal of Horse, for example, was a sergeant in the cavalry. If a soldier was a private, trooper, sapper or gunner, he was usually at the bottom of the promotion ladder, any other rank being further up it!

This is a very simplified table. Various branches and regiments have tended to give different names to different ranks. For example, in the Royal Artillery a Private is called a Gunner, in the Royal Engineers he is a Sapper, and in Cavalry regiments he may be called a Trooper.

Appendix 3

Useful Dates

Records of units and formations engaged in particular campaigns are listed in detail in M Roper's *Records of the War Office and related departments 1660-1964* (PRO Handbook No 29, 1998).

Campaigns and wars

1642-1649	English Civil War
1660 May 25	Restoration of Charles I
1688	Glorious Revolution
1701-1713	War of Spanish Succession
1704 Aug 13	Battle of Blenheim
1715	Jacobite Rebellion
1740-1748	War of Austrian Succession
1745	Jacobite Rebellion
1756 May 3 - 1763 Feb 10	Seven Years War
1775-1783	American War of Independence
1789	French Revolution
1793 Feb 1 - 1815 Jun 22	Napoleonic Wars (or French Revolutionary Wars)
1808 Aug 1 - 1814 Mar 30	Peninsular Campaign
1815 Jun 18	Battle of Waterloo
1812 Jun 19 - 1815 Jan 8	Second Anglo-American War (War of 1812)
1854 Sept 14 - 1856 Mar 30	Crimean War
1854 Oct 25	Charge of the Light Brigade
1857 May 10 - Dec 6	Indian Mutiny
1860, 1862-1864	Maori Wars in New Zealand
1878-1879	Zulu War
1879 Jan 22	Massacre of British Troops at Isandhlwana, Zululand

1878-1881	First South African (Boer) War
1881 Feb 27	Defeat of British troops at Majuba Hill, South Africa
1882-1885	Egyptian and Sudan Campaigns
1885 Jan 29	Relief of Khartoum
1898	Sudan campaign
1899 Oct 12 - 1902 May 31	Second South African (Boer) War
1900 Feb 28	Relief of Ladysmith, South Africa
1900 May 17	Relief of Mafeking, South Africa
1914 Aug 4 - 1918 Nov 11	First World War
1914 Aug 22-23	Battle of Mons
1915 Apr 25 - 1916 Jan 8	Gallipoli campaign, Turkey
1916 July 1 - Nov 8	Battle of the Somme
1917 Jul 31 - Nov 10	Battle of Passchendaele (Third Battle of Ypres)
1916 Apr 24 - May 1	Easter Rising, Dublin
1922 Dec 17	Last British troops leave Southern Ireland
1939 Sept 3 - 1945 Sept 2	Second World War
1940 May 27 - June 4	Evacuation from Dunkirk
1941 Apr 22 - May 29	Greek and Crete campaigns
1942 Feb 15	Surrender of Singapore
1942 Oct 23	Start of Battle of El Alamein
1943 Jul 10	Allies land in Sicily
1944 Jun 6	Allies land in France (D-Day)
1945 May 8	Germans surrender (VE-Day)
1945 Aug 14	Surrender of Japan (VJ-Day)
1947 Aug 15	Last British troops leave India
1948 May 14	Last British troops leave Palestine
1950 Jun 26 - 1953 Jul 27	Korean War
1956 Oct 31 - Nov 7	Suez Crisis

Army history

1645	Formation of New Model Army
1661	Britain's oldest regiment, the Coldstream Guards, formed

1664	Royal Marines established
1684	Admission of first pensioners to the Royal Hospital Kilmainham, Ireland
1692	Admission of first pensioners to the Royal Hospital Chelsea
1708	Provision of pensions to widows of officers
1716	Royal Artillery founded
1717	Corps of Engineers founded
1740	First publication of the Army List
1757	Militia Act revives local militias
1760	Institution of soldiers' pension documents
1787	Corps of Engineers becomes Royal Engineers
1796	Establishment of Army Chaplains Department
1810	Army Medical Department established
1811	Royal Corps of Sappers and Miners set up
1833	Long Service and Good Conduct Medal instituted
1839-1915	Hart's Army Lists
1854	Institution of Distinguished Conduct Medal
1855	Ordnance Board abolished
1856	Victoria Cross instituted
1857	Army Hospital Corps formed
1859	Volunteer regiments formed
1867	Second Class Army Reserve established
1870	Army Enlistment Act introduces of short service engagements of 12 years for other ranks
1870	Abolition of purchase of commission
1881	Abolition of numbered regiments of foot and their re-establishment as regiments with county affiliations
1881	Army Nursing Service formed
1886	Institution of Distinguished Service Order
1898	Royal Army Medical Corps formed by merger of Army Medical Department and Army Medical Staff Corps
1918	Formation of Royal Air Force from Royal Flying Corps and Royal Naval Air Service
1922	Irish regiments disbanded on independence of Irish Free State
1940-1944	Home Guard (Local Defence Volunteers)

APPENDIX 4

Records Held by other Institutions

Local record offices

Relatively few military records are held by local record offices. Those that are, however, are often of great interest to the family historian. Three different types of military records may be held by a local record office.

Firstly, there are records created by local units, either volunteers or the regular army. These may consist of service rolls, war diaries and internal records of the unit and can give an insight into the life of the service. Records of some territorial and auxiliary forces associations have been deposited at local record offices and may contain items of interest to family historians. Details of these records, for the First World War period, are in Norman Holding, *The Location of British Army Records: a National Directory of World War I Sources* (FFHS, 1991).

Local record offices also hold records of local militia units. In particular, militia lists (of all men) and militia enrolment lists (of men chosen to serve) may survive for the period 1758 to 1831. These records, and others likely to be of use to the family historian, are described in Jeremy Gibson and Mervyn Medlycott, *Militia Lists and Musters, 1757-1876* (FFHS, 1990).

Records relating to military events, although not military records as such, include rolls of honour for men who served during the world wars, or lists of casualties taken from local newspapers. Photographs of parades and manoeuvres may also be held locally.

Brief details of the holdings of most record repositories in Britain are given in Janet Foster and Julia Sheppard, *British archives: a guide to archive resources in the United Kingdom* (2nd edition, 1988). The addresses of local record offices, together with times of opening, are given in *Record Repositories in Great Britain* (10th edition, PRO, 1997). Similar information is included in Jeremy Gibson, *Record offices: how to find them* (FFHS, 1991), together with maps and other details.

National Register of Archives

The National Register of Archives (NRA) was set up by the Royal Commission on Historical Manuscripts in 1945 to collect and disseminate information about manuscript sources for British history outside public records. The NRA consists of more than 40,000 unpublished lists and catalogues of major collections. They describe the holdings of local record offices, national and university, and other specialist repositories. Many of these collections may contain records of use to the family or military historian.

An index to these lists and catalogues is available in the reading room and can also be accessed via the Internet. The NRA also publish a useful free leaflet, *Sources for the History of the Armed Forces* (NRA Information Sheet no 8), which lists many of the major sources for military records.

> National Register of Archives
> Royal Commission on Historical Manuscripts
> Quality House
> Quality Court
> Chancery Lane
> London
> WC2A 1HP
> (0171-242 1198)
> http://www.hmc.gov.uk

Imperial War Museum

The Imperial War Museum has a very large collection of private diaries, letters, papers and unpublished memoirs for all ranks in the Army from 1914 to the present and a large photographic library. These can be consulted by appointment. The Museum also maintains a comprehensive series of biographical files on persons decorated with the Victoria Cross or the George Cross since the inception of the awards. The address is:

> Imperial War Museum
> Lambeth Road
> London
> SE1 6HZ
> (0171-416 5000)
> http://www.iwm.org.uk

British Library, Oriental and India Office Collections (formerly India Office Library and Records (IOLR))

The IOLR hold very large collections of material relating to the British in India. They also hold 1,000 volumes of births, marriages and deaths returns between c 1683 and 1947. There are indexes to these records.

Further information about their holdings of use to the genealogist may be found in Ian A Baxter, *A brief guide to biographical sources*, produced by the IOLR in 1979. The address is:

> British Library, Oriental and India Office Collections
> 197 Blackfriars Road
> London
> SE1 8NG
> (0171-412 7873)
> http://www.bl.uk

It will be moving to the main British Library site at 96 Euston Road, St Pancras, London NW1 2DB in 1998-1999.

National Army Museum

The Museum has a large collection of private, regimental and related papers concerning the British Army, the Indian Army prior to 1947, and British colonial forces to relevant dates of independence.

The life of the ordinary soldier is well illustrated by letters, diaries, memoirs and poems written by men stationed in every corner of the globe. There is a fine representative collection of commissions of officers for both the British and Indian armies.

The Museum holds regimental records for the 9th/12th Royal Lancers, Westminster Dragoons, Surrey Yeomanry, and various Indian Army units, together with documents relating to the Irish regiments of the British Army disbanded upon the formation of the Irish Free State in 1922: the Royal Irish Regiment, Connaught Rangers (materials relating to the history of the Connaught Rangers, 1793-1916, are also held at the Public Record Office in WO 79), Leinster Regiment, Royal Munster Fusiliers, and the Royal Dublin Fusiliers. Of particular interest to the family historian is the card index of biographical information on officers of the East India Company compiled by Major Vernon Hodson.

In addition, it holds a comprehensive record of all military casualties from 1900 to the present day, giving next of kin, address and how personal possessions and money were dispersed.

The Museum also has a very large library of regimental histories, military biographies and Army Lists, together with collections of photographs and sound recordings of old soldiers. The address is:

> National Army Museum
> Royal Hospital Road
> London
> SW3 4HT
> (0171-730 0717)
> http://www.failte.com/nam/

Regimental Museums

Many regiments have a museum, some of which have collections of records which could be of use to the family historian.

T Wise and S Wise, *A guide to military museums and other places of military interest* (8th edition, 1994) gives the addresses of museums with a brief description of their collections. In addition, Norman Holding, *The location of British Army records* (FFHS, 1991) lists museums and gives some idea of the records that each one holds relating to the First World War although these may have been deposited with.

Office for National Statistics (General Register Office)

The history of Army registration of births, marriages and deaths is not quite clear. Most of the records held by the General Register Office cannot be inspected by the public although indexes may be seen at the Family Records Centre, 1 Myddelton Street, London EC1R 1UW. Once you have identified a relevant entry from the indexes you may order a copy of the entry as an official certificate for a fee. A few Army registers or records of births, marriages and deaths are in the PRO (see section 19.1); others may still be in the custody of the regiment.

The General Register Office has registers of Army births and marriages from 1761 to 1987, and of deaths from 1796 to 1987. There are several series, some of them overlapping, with an uncertain amount of duplication and omission. The regimental registers of births/baptisms and marriages run from 1761 to 1924, covering events in Britain (from 1761) and abroad (from c 1790). There is an index to the births (giving name, place, year and regiment), but not to the marriages. To find out details of a marriage, you have to know the husband's regiment and a rough date. At the FRC is a list of the marriage registers, arranged by regiment: if your regiment is there, with entries for the right period, ask at the enquiry desk in the FRC to be put in touch with the Overseas Section, which may conduct a search for you.

Overlapping with the regimental registers are the Army chaplains' returns of births, baptisms, marriages, deaths and burials, 1796-1880. These all relate to events abroad, and they are indexed. Unfortunately, the indexes do not give the regiment, simply name, place and date range. From 1881 they appear to be continued by the Army returns, 1881-1955, of births, marriages and deaths overseas. From 1920, entries relating to the Royal Air Force are included.

From 1956-1965, there are indexes to combined service department registers of births and marriages overseas: after 1965, separate service registers were abandoned, and entries were made in the general series of overseas registers.

Records for the Ionian Islands appear to have been kept separately. At the FRC there are registers, 1818-1864, of births, marriages and deaths: the index is to a military register, a civil register, and a chaplain's register. It gives names only. Other registers from the Ionian Islands are in the PRO; the register for Zante gives baptisms, marriages, deaths and burials 1849-1859 (RG 33/82).

Fees, similar to those charged for copies of ordinary certificates, are payable. The address for postal enquiries is:

> Office for National Statistics
> General Register Office (Postal Application Section)
> Smedley Hydro
> Trafalgar Road
> Birkdale
> Southport
> Merseyside
> PR8 2HH
> (0151-471 4816)

Scotland

Census returns and certain registers relating to deaths of warrant officers, NCOs and men in the South African War (1899-1902) are held at the General Register Office for Scotland, New Register House, Edinburgh EH1 3YT. They also hold an incomplete set of birth, marriage and death registers for Scottish armed forces for the Second World War.

It may be possible to trace the present whereabouts of regimental collections through the Scottish United Services Museum, The Castle, Edinburgh EH1 2NG.

Ireland

Most nineteenth century census records relating to Ireland have not survived but census returns for 1901 and 1911 may be consulted at the National Archives of Ireland, Bishop Street, Dublin 8, Ireland.

Birth, marriage and death registers created under the Army Act 1879 for the period between 1880 and 1921 are held by the General Register Office, Joyce House, 8-11 Lombard Street, Dublin 2.

Society of Genealogists

The library of the Society has a number of useful books, including regimental histories and rolls of honour. In addition, the Society has produced leaflets on *Army muster and description books*, *Army research: selected bibliography* and *In search of a soldier ancestor*. The address is:

> Society of Genealogists
> 14 Charterhouse Buildings
> Goswell Road
> London
> EC1M 7BA
> (0171-251 8799)

APPENDIX 5

Further Reading

The best general introduction to family history in the Public Record Office is Amanda Bevan's revised edition of *Tracing Your Ancestors in the Public Record Office* (5th edition, PRO, 1999). Section 18 in the book covers many of the classes of military records of genealogical interest in the PRO.

The Office also produces a number of Records Information Leaflets on many subjects of interest to the family historian. The leaflets are intended to be used at the PRO in conjunction with the records. They are available free of charge to those visiting the Office. The PRO is unable to supply leaflets by post. The leaflets are continually evolving and new leaflets are always being produced. Please ask at the Research Enquiries Room.

In addition, there are a number of source sheets which aim to provide searchers with lists of references on popular topics.

Stella Colwell, *Family Roots* (London, 1991) gives many examples of military records to be found at the PRO and includes a brief account of finding ancestors who served in the Army. An idiosyncratic account of how to trace individuals in Army records is Gerald Hamilton-Edwards, *In Search of Army Ancestry* (Chichester, 1977). The Society of Genealogists will shortly be publishing Michael J Watts, *My Ancestor was in the British Army - How can I find out more about him?* R H Montague, *How to trace your military ancestors in Australia and New Zealand* (Sydney, 1989) is a useful illustrated guide to military records of value to genealogists in Australia and New Zealand. Many queries about military records are answered in F C Markwell and Pauline Saul, *The family historian's enquire within* (3rd edition, FFHS, 1991).

There are several general histories of the British Army which can provide background information for the family historian, such as David Ascoli, *A Companion to the British Army, 1660-1983* (London, 1983). A useful introduction to the organization of the Army before 1914 is given in John M Kitzmiller II, *In Search of the 'Forlorn Hope': a Comprehensive Guide to Locating British Regiments and their Records, 1640 to World War One* (2 vols, Salt Lake City, 1988). A good general history of the British Army is Corelli Barnett, *Britain and her army* (London, 1970).

An interesting account of the life of the soldier is Victor Neuburg, *Gone for a soldier* (London, 1989). Byron Farwell, *For queen and country: a social history of the Victorian and Edwardian army* (London, 1981) is a well written introduction to the life many ancestors must have experienced. A pictorial introduction to the life of the Scottish soldier is Jenni Calder, *The story of the Scottish soldier, 1600-1914* (HMSO, 1987).

General works

D Ascoli, *A Companion to the British Army, 1660-1983* (London, 1983)

D J Barnes, 'Identification and Dating: Military Uniforms', in *Family History Focus*, ed, D J Steel and L Taylor (Guildford, 1984)

A P Bruce, *An Annotated Bibliography of the British Army, 1660-1714* (London, 1975)

P Dennis, *The Terrtiorial Army 1907-1940* (Royal Historical Society, 1987)

C Firth and G Davis, *The Regimental History of Cromwell's Army* (Oxford, 1940)

Y Fitzmaurice, *Army Deserters from HM Service* (Forest Hill, Victoria, 1988)

S Fowler, W Spencer and S Tamblin, *Army Service Records of the First World War* (PRO Readers' Guide No 19, London, 1997)

J Gibson and A Dell, *Tudor and Stuart Muster Rolls* (FFHS, 1991)

J Gibson and M Medlycott, *Militia Lists and Musters, 1757-1876* (FFHS, 1994)

G Hamilton-Edwards, *In Search of Army Ancestry* (London, 1977)

N Holding, *The Location of British Army Records: a National Directory of World War One Sources* (FFHS, 3rd edn, 1991)

N Holding, *More Sources of World War One Army Ancestry* (FFHS, 1991)

N Holding, *World War One Army Ancestry* (FFHS, 1997)

J M Kitzmiller II, *In Search of the 'Forlorn Hope': a Comprehensive Guide to Locating British Regiments and their Records 1640 to World War One* (Salt Lake City, 1988)

M E S Laws, *Battery Records of the Royal Artillery, 1716-1877* (Woolwich, 1952-1970)

M Medlycott, 'Some Georgian 'Censuses': the Militia Lists and 'Defence' Lists', *Genealogists' Magazine*, vol XXIII, pp 55-59

Public Record Office, *Alphabetical Guide to certain War Office and other Military Records preserved in the Public Record Office* (PRO Lists and Indexes, vol LXIII)

Public Record Office, *First World War: Indexes to Medal Entitlement* (Information Leaflet)

Public Record Office, *Lists of War Office Records* (Lists and Indexes, vol XXVIII and Supplementary vol VIII)

Public Record Office, *Nurses and the Nursing Services: Record Sources in the Public Record Office* (Information Leaflet)

Public Record Office, *Records of Courts Martial: Army* (Information Leaflet)

Public Record Office, *Records of Medals* (Information Leaflet)

Public Record Office, *Service Medal and Award Rolls: War of 1914-1918* (WO 329) (Information Leaflet)

E E Rich, 'The Population of Elizabethan England', *Economic History Review,* 2nd ser, vol II, pp 247-265(Discusses the Elizabethan muster rolls)

W Spencer, *Records of the Militia and Volunteer Forces 1757-1945* (London, 1997)

A Swinson ed, *A Register of the Regiments and Corps of the British Army: the Ancestry of the Regiments and Corps of the Regular Establishments of the Army* (London, 1975)

C T Watts and M J Watts, 'In Search of a Soldier Ancestor', *Genealogists' Magazine,* vol XIX, pp 125-128

A S White, *A Bibliography of the Regiments and Corps of the British Army* (London, 1965)

T Wise and S Wise, *A Guide to Military Museums and Other Places of Military Interest* (Doncaster, 8th edn, 1994)

PRO publications, and those of the Federation of Family History Societies (FFHS), are on sale at the PRO shops at Kew and the Family Records Centre.

Index